A Little Girl's
WAR

WENDY APPLETON

AMBERLEY

First published 2012

Amberley Publishing
The Hill, Stroud
Gloucestershire, GL5 4EP

www.amberleybooks.com

British Library Cataloguing in Publication Data.
A catalogue record for this book is available from the British Library.

ISBN 978 1 4456 0639 2

Typesetting and Origination by Amberley Publishing.
Printed in Great Britain.

CONTENTS

In Memory of my parents, Arthur and Doris Cawley,
also sisters Sheila and Betty
and to my other sister and brothers,
Thelma, Brian, David and Christopher.

And also my husband Brian,
my children and their spouses,
Nigel and Vicki, Debra and Krys,
and Grandchildren Matthew and Minnie.

CHAPTER 1

A Little Girl at Home

Brian and Wendy outside the shelter in
the early years of the war.

I can remember as if it were yesterday. That spring day back in 1944. In a small infant school in Kent, the Garden of England they called it, where, in orchard upon orchard, apples, pears, plums and cherries grew in abundance. (We would drape the twin ruby-coloured cherries over our ears as earrings.)

The sheep grazed peacefully among the awakened fruit trees, now clothed in blossom, happy to feel at last the warming rays of the sun after the chill of a long grey winter. Soft, creamy newborn lambs, long tails shaking with delight, guzzled their mothers' milk, or chased and gambolled together, then suddenly leaping into the air with the sheer joy of being alive. Pink and white blossoms blown by the wind sent petals falling and drifting like confetti to the fresh, damp emerald grass beneath. Blackbirds perched in the branches of the fruit trees singing, their shining black feathered breasts puffed out towards the clear blue sky above, hoping to attract their dull brown mate sitting in the next tree.

Huge grey-white cumulous clouds gathered, bringing the promise of another short sharp shower to wet the grass yet again, and to bring fresh life to the once winter-dormant trees and flowers.

The bees buzzing amongst the apple blossoms paused to gather nectar from each small clump of pale yellow primroses, growing around the trunks of the trees, looking just like blobs of cream among the fresh, quilted leaves. The whole countryside, now full of life, was shaking off the dull days of winter. Ah, spring is here at last!

In the kindergarten class, my teacher Miss Fisher, who wore glasses and had her hair in a tight bun, looking every inch the typical teacher, was just getting into her stride with the simple addition maths lesson. There were posters on the walls of our classroom with numbers one to ten beside domino dots in the same amount. We found it very helpful to count on our fingers. Four neat rows of six small tables and chairs faced the front of the class and the blackboard.

We did our sums, writing them in our exercise books, and then we formed a line, one behind the other, to get our work marked by our teacher, who sat at her desk trying to drum into our heads the theory, and just where we had gone wrong. I stood behind a blonde tousle-headed boy, Roger Edgington; he was wearing a Fair Isle sleeveless pullover and was making rude noises, blowing raspberries and making us laugh, so much so that one little girl wet her pants and made a puddle on the floor. Just as we were about to tell our teacher, the loud wailing of the air-raid siren warned us of an imminent bombing attack. (Jenny Markham was going to have to stay in her wet pants.)

Miss Fisher grabbed her brown leather bag and boxed gas mask from her desk as we all began to hurry for the door, following the drill for the imminent air raid, at the same time grabbing our gas masks off their hooks by the door.

'Quick, all of you, one at a time now, down to the shelter; no, not you Wendy,' she added, as I passed her. 'You might as well just run home, you haven't got far to go and it will soon be home time anyway.'

My teacher was tired, after yet another sleepless night, with an almost non-stop bombardment of enemy bombs the night before. If she had stopped to think, she would have realised that it was not a good idea to send a five-year-old child home during an air raid, but her thoughts were on other things as she shepherded the rest of her pupils towards the door.

The other children, as they had been taught to do, carrying their gas masks, ran quickly across the small playground, to the wide stone steps on the field, near the entrance gate to the school. The steps led down to the underground shelter. Then, pushing and stumbling down the concrete steps, the children found themselves inside the cold, stark grey walls of the air-raid shelter, where the bare light bulbs hung dimly, casting weird shadows on the concrete block walls. With anxious faces, they sat down on the row of wooden benches lining the walls. Quickly, the rest of the school children joined them. The dirty walls were hung with cobwebs and the whole place smelt of pee. But they were used to it and so it went unnoticed. A blackboard and easel, complete with chalk, stood at one end ready for their underground lessons.

I grabbed my coat and gas mask, happy not to have to go down to that smelly shelter again where we seemed to spend hours singing:

Ten green bottles hanging on the wall,
Ten green bottles hanging on the wall,

And if one green bottle should accidentally fall,
There'd be nine green bottles hanging on the wall.

On and on we would sing the song until, at the end when,

There'd be nothing but the sme-ell, a-hanging on the wall!

We sang at the tops of our young voices, trying to drown the noise of the guns and bombs outside, and to keep our spirits up. For us it was all we had ever known. From the year after we were born. Since 1939, England and many other countries had been at war with Germany.

But for now, I ran across the playground and, turning the corner of the one-storey school building, I scampered down the narrow shrub-lined alley beside the school that led to Pelham Road, the road where I lived. Long rows of terraced houses stretched on either side of the road before me. Side by side in groups of four, the small three-bedroom homes looked all alike with their square pocket-handkerchief front gardens, bay windows and small tiled porch roofs above the front door.

The wailing of the undulating warning siren frightened me. I had learned to be scared of that sound and all that it meant. Ominous grey clouds gathered overhead and it started to rain. I paused and looked up. High in the sky above me, I could see three tiny planes, two British Spitfires and a German Messerschmitt, battling it out, their guns blazing.

Feeling scared, and very alone, I began to cry, my tears now mingling with the drops of rain falling down my cheeks. Starting to run faster, my small brown buttoned shoes tap-tapped a rhythm on the pavement as I ran, while my boxed gas mask beat a new rhythm on my hip. My thin legs were soon splashed with mud. I ran faster; I was terrified. Supposing the planes should shoot at me? It had never seemed such a long journey home from school.

By the time I reached my gate, I had slowed down somewhat as I was wheezing from an asthma attack. The once crisp, white bow in my short brown hair hung down, limply. Trying to walk more quickly, I approached our brown front door and rattled and banged the doorknocker, shouting for my mother, my voice rising to a scream as I saw one of the Spitfires spiralling out of the sky, leaving a plume of smoke trailing behind it. It landed with a loud explosion on the school field at the other end of the road, dissolving into flames. The young nineteen- or twenty-year-old pilot had met his fate.

'Mummy, let me in!' I shouted. There was no reply. I leaned on the door trying to get my breath, when suddenly it burst open and my eldest sister stood there holding a glass baby's feeding bottle in her hand. In one glance she took in the state of me, and putting her free arm around my waist, and shutting the door behind me, she half carried, half dragged me into the house. Through the narrow hall and the kitchen and out of the back door, my feet barely touching the floor, to the Anderson air-raid shelter that we had buried in the back garden. Then, she almost threw me down the wooden ladder. I found myself in a crumpled heap on the dirt floor.

As my eyes became accustomed to the gloom I saw my mother sitting on a bunk at the other end nursing my baby brother Christopher. My sister Sheila climbed down after me and handed Mummy the baby's bottle she had retrieved from the house. She nodded towards me. 'Look who I found,' she said. My mother had a scarf tied turban style around her hair, which she still had in curlers from when she had washed it earlier. She wore an old brown cardigan, fastened with a large safety pin, over her apron. The cardigan had seen better days with a few hurriedly darned holes in it. She pulled up her sleeve and tested the heat of the baby's milk on the inside of her wrist. When the air raid started, both my mother and Sheila had rushed outside to the shelter with the babies, forgetting that the baby's feed had been left behind. Sheila had bravely ventured back inside the house to retrieve it, and it was very lucky for me that she had!

I adored my nineteen-year-old sister; she was very pretty with a lovely smile. She wore her hair curled in a roll at the front and the rest was caught up at the sides and fastened at the nape of her neck, in a snood or small net. Feeling grateful that she should have found me, I gave her a watery smile.

'What is your teacher thinking about, sending you home in the middle of an air raid?' Sheila asked me.

My mother looked up. 'She should know better. Are you all right, dear?' she added, looking very concerned as I tried to breathe.

My shoulders were hunched up to make it easier. I sat beside her, wiping my wet face on my dripping coat sleeve. My chest felt as though it would burst as I wheezed and struggled to breathe out, the effort shaking my thin body, and making me feel weak. Wriggling out of my coat, I let it drop to the floor. My mother, still cradling the baby, bent down and grabbed it. She hung the coat on one of the bunk posts. Sheila meanwhile reached for a small bottle of white ephedrine hydrochloride tablets, and pouring water into a glass from the water decanter on the small table by her bunk, she handed me a tablet and the water to wash it down.

I was quite used to this remedy and dutifully took it and swallowed the water, and then I looked around the shelter. There were two bunks with dark grey blankets on them, one above the other on each long side of the cold grey corrugated-iron walls and two smaller ones at the far end. One of the smaller ones had a baby's gas mask on it. It looked like a grey torpedo and was shaped so that the baby could be placed inside. There was a pump to allow you to pump the fresh air to the inside. Christopher, my baby brother, hated it; he would kick up such a fuss if we attempted to place him in it.

As I leaned across and kissed my tiny brother's soft fuzzy golden head, I wrinkled up my nose. 'He needs changing, Mummy,' I said. Sheila reached in a cloth bag for yet another terry towelling nappy, handing it to my mother together with a jar of Vaseline, and a tin of baby powder. Mummy placed the baby on the bunk beside her and began changing his smelly nappy, which she dropped into an enamel pail on the floor beside her. The sweet stinky smell filled the air-raid shelter. I held my nose.

As my mother continued to feed Christopher, the anti-aircraft guns continued their firing outside and then there was an almighty bang. I jumped and Christopher began to cry, a loud complaining cry; he didn't like the noise. To add to the cacophony, another small wail was heard. The tousled head of my three-year-old brother David appeared from under the rumpled, torn, grey blanket on the top bunk opposite. I had forgotten about him. David sat up shaking, his eyes wide and frightened, looking about him, then swinging his little legs over the side of the bunk he held out his skinny arms to Sheila as a huge tear plopped on the earthy floor. He whimpered as she took him in her arms and one of his small white socks fell off. 'Come on,' she said, plonking a kiss on his head and cuddling him in her arms, 'those nasty old Germans, let's sing a song,' and jogging him up and down on her knee she burst into

> Oh we ain't got a barrel of money,
> Maybe we're ragged and funny,
> But we travel along,
> Singing a song
> Side by side.

Mummy joined in:

> Don't know what's coming tomorrow,
> Maybe it's trouble and sorrow,
> But we travel the road,
> Sharing our load,
> Side by side.

> Thru all kinds of weather,
> What if the sky should fall?
> But as long as we're together
> It really doesn't matter at all.

When we've all had our troubles and parted
We'll be the same as we started,
Just travelling the road
Sharing our load
Side by side.

David gave a watery grin and rubbed his eyes; he turned his head away as Sheila tried to wipe his runny nose. Christopher, now smelling sweeter after being changed, and powdered, went back hungrily to his bottle. I smiled at the noises he made as he fed. It was good to be home! The guns rumbled outside but we were safe! Or so I thought.

Soon we heard the 'all clear' siren sounding and as we stumbled up the ladder, I followed close behind Sheila, who still carried David, while Mummy brought up the rear with the baby. We all emerged blinking, into the now-brilliant sunshine; I looked up into the grey-blue sky, eyeing the barrage balloon overhead. 'Good,' I thought to myself, 'the planes have all gone.' Then I saw a wonderful rainbow hanging in the sky. 'Red and yellow, and pink and green ...' I sang to myself and turned to look at Sheila as she put David down, and I heard her gasp.

Following her gaze to just beyond the end of our long narrow garden, behind the tall wooden fence that separated our garden from the back alley, we found ourselves staring at a pile of burning rubble, once a house. Now all that was left amongst the rubble were the wooden stairs pointing skywards, now going nowhere. As the sound of the fire engine was heard, its bell ringing urgently, Mummy shrugged her shoulders and said resignedly, 'There is nothing we can do, let's get indoors.' So with a tired but determined look on her face, she turned and carried the baby, and with David now clinging to her skirt with one hand and sucking his other thumb, we entered the kitchen to a really horrid, acrid smell.

At first we thought our house was on fire too, being met by clouds of evil-smelling steam and smoke pouring out of the open kitchen door. A saucepan of potato peelings on the stove had boiled dry; the smoke, steam and stench now filled the kitchen. 'Oh darn,' said my mother, 'I forgot about those.' When the air-raid siren went, she had been boiling up the potato peelings for the hens, which we kept so that we could have fresh eggs. The peelings were then mixed with a handful of meal and fed to the chickens. They really loved this mix and would come running as we filled their trough.

Mummy quickly handed the baby to Sheila, and taking a thick cloth, she grabbed the pan and flung it into the sink, at the same time turning on the tap to a loud hissing. My mother looked crossly at the black mess in the bottom of the pan. What could she give the hens now?

Sheila took the baby upstairs for a nap, while I drew a smiling face in the steam on the kitchen window. David started to grizzle with the lack of attention. He was still half asleep having been so rudely awakened and it was making him crabby. I stopped drawing on the window. 'I'm hungry, Mummy,' I said.

'You are always hungry,' she replied with a sigh. Turning from the burnt pan in the sink, she took a chipped white china pudding basin from the larder, and then began to scrape some of the beef dripping from it onto a crust of bread. Adding as a topping a scraping of Marmite, she cut the crust in half and handed one piece to David and the other to me. David almost choked as, hungrily, he tried to push it all into his small mouth at once. He began to cough, spraying me with breadcrumbs, and started to cry all over again.

I took no notice and bit into my half of the crust and with dripping around my mouth, and trickling down my chin, I munched hungrily gazing around the kitchen. It was a small room about 9 feet square. The walls were painted with a dull matt green distemper. A single frosted-glass white Coolie-shaped lampshade hung from the centre of the ceiling revealing the naked light bulb within. The gas stove stood by the door to the hall. It had an eye-level grill with a plate rack either side and was enamelled a grey-blue colour. We kept the broom in the corner next to it. On the other side of the stove stood a small boiler that was fed with coke from the tall enamel hod beside it; this heated our water. Above the boiler was a wooden clothes airer, which descended by pulley from the ceiling. It was now filled with damp, threadbare grey nappies that added to the steamy atmosphere of the kitchen.

The chipped ceramic white sink was situated under the window with a wooden dish drainer beside it. Under the sink was a grey enamel bucket with an evil-smelling floor cloth inside. The cloth was used for any spills made on the floor (which had bare floorboards) and sometimes didn't get rinsed out very well because, if you squeezed the cloth, you could get splinters in your fingers from the floor. I had gained a few to prove it. On the other wall, beside the back door, was a brown varnished door leading to a built-in larder, containing a wooden rack for eggs and a marble slab to keep the butter and cheese cool (when we had some). There were shelves of Mummy's homemade jams and preserves, and several neatly stacked large oval meat dishes in a blue and white willow pattern.

Outside the back door in the garden, beneath the rusty corrugated roof overhang supported by a piece of four-by-four timber, was a green metal mangle with two hard rubber rollers for squeezing the water out of the laundry. On washdays I would help Mummy by passing the clothes to her from a tin baby bath. Once, when I tried to put the sheets through the mangle I caught my fingers in it. How I yelled as I tried to suck away the pain. Once the water was squeezed out, Mother would then proceed to hang up the clothes with wooden clothes pins purchased from a gypsy who had knocked on our door. You couldn't refuse a gypsy or she might put a curse on you! Besides we could always use more clothes pegs; they seemed to disappear mysteriously. The long clothes line stretched to the end of the garden and a wooden pole was used to prop up the line when it was full.

Sometimes the washing was too heavy for the clothes line and it would snap under the weight. Then we had to gather up the clothes and wash them all over again! On those days it was a good idea to get lost! My mother wasn't in a very good mood if that happened.

I remember one day I was standing by the kitchen sink, my head and shoulders just above the rim of it, watching my mother rubbing the endless stained baby's nappies against her metal washboard. Her hands red and sore as she wheezed with an asthma attack and the effort, her face pink and her brown hair falling forward. Thinking for a moment, I looked up into her face and said seriously, 'Why don't people believe that God makes babies?' I paused. 'How else do they think they would get here?'

My mother stared at me and said, 'Out of the mouths of babes.'

But I was already thinking of something else. Above the mangle was our wooden meat safe, hanging on the fence. The door of which was covered with fine wire mesh. We kept the meat in here for a while until one day my father discovered a joint of ham covered in ants. He brought the ham indoors and washed it under the tap. 'There,' he said, beaming, 'good as new!' I wasn't so sure, but we were always hungry so we ate it.

Beneath the larder was another cupboard that housed the gas meter. We had to 'feed' it with shillings to stop the gas from being cut off. The root vegetables were also kept in a dirty old earthy-smelling shopping bag in there. We had a similar meter for the electric, which was housed in the hall cupboard under the stairs. Sometimes the light went off when it had run out and we would scurry around in the dark, trying to find a shilling. On the days that the meter man came to empty the meter, my mother would beam if he gave her some shillings back because we had put too many in. She kept them in a black tin with a slit in the lid, but those days were rare.

The next cupboard in the kitchen was where we kept the saucepans and plates, together with tinned products, when they were available. Above this on the wall hung a beautifully carved and polished 2-foot-long, mahogany wall clock with Big Ben chimes. It was Father's pride and joy and he would wind the clock up every Sunday night, ready for the following week. I found the sound of the chimes somehow comforting.

The kitchen cabinet stood against the last wall opposite the window. It was painted cream and green. There was a cupboard at the bottom for baking tins and bowls, then a drawer, which held our cutlery, and finally the centre door opened downwards to make a worktop for pastry making. It had a white enamel surface to keep the pastry cool. On the left inside was a square metal container for flour; it had a knob which, when pulled back and forth, would sift the lumps from the flour as it poured. On the right of the flour container was a shelf where my mother kept one of her most prized possessions. It was a large blue hardback copy of *Mrs Beeton's Cookery Book*. Written in better days when it was easy to find the extravagant ingredients.

Mummy now removed her old brown cardigan, hung it on the kitchen doorknob, rolled up her sleeves and then opened the book to read, 'Take six eggs ...' 'Now wouldn't that be nice,' she must have thought to herself.

In the early days when my parents, Doris and Arthur, were first married, they had lived in Welwyn Garden City and were able to afford both a cook and a nanny for their first two daughters, Sheila Mary and Betty Marion. Then the twins, Thelma Anne and Diane Cecelia, arrived and times changed. The money became scarce. Two more mouths to feed made a lot of difference. There were Mummy's pills to pay for, then as each new baby arrived, my parents' fleeting affluence became a thing of the past. Their first son was born next and they named him Brian Aubrey John (after my grandfather). They then moved to Woolwich Road in

Bexleyheath, which was where I, Wendy Judith, was born. They moved again to Pelham Road and Mummy gave birth to another boy, David Arthur, and finally Christopher Michael arrived and our family was complete.

Now my mother turned to a large tin of 'National dried egg', which was all most people could get in those days. We had been lucky in owning our own hens. But even then, there were days when they wouldn't lay; so then we used the dried egg, but in any case it made really nice scrambled eggs, so it wasn't too much of a hardship – except that we had to pay for it of course!

There was a knock at the front door and I ran to open it. Banging my knee on the black triangular umbrella stand that stood in the corner by the door, I rubbed my bruised leg and then, stretching up on my tiptoes, I turned the small oval brass doorknob; it was stiff and cut into my fingers. There stood my older brother Brian. A little taller than me, he wore his jumper tied round his middle by the sleeves. The top button of his raincoat was buttoned at the neck. He wore it like a cape. His grey school cap was stuffed in his pocket and a lock of hair on the crown of his head stood up to attention. His face was dirty and his skinny legs stuck out from scruffy knee-length pants, his long grey socks, above his black muddy lace-up shoes, were at half mast around his ankles. He was eight years old.

'Guess what I've got,' he said, stretching his fist above his head so that I couldn't reach it.

'Oh, let's see,' I begged, grabbing at his arm and treading on his feet in my eagerness.

'Ouch!' He relented and opened his hand to reveal an ugly piece of grey metal. 'Shrapnel!' he announced proudly.

'Guess what! There is a crashed airplane in our school field.'

'I know. I watched it come down.' I said it in a singsong voice, feeling important that I had seen it before him, at once forgetting how scared I had been as I watched it spiral down out of control.

Brian had found the piece of shattered bomb casing on the way home from school. All the children prized these pieces of scorched twisted metal and would keep boxes of them to swap with each other. It was a sort of trophy to be taken out of the box and gazed at and wondered about from time to time. Brian took off his raincoat, slinging it over the banisters, and walked into the kitchen, still holding the shrapnel tightly in his hand.

'What's for tea, Mum?' he asked.

'Nothing for you until you wash your hands, and throw that junk away,' she added with a look of distaste, at the same time going and removing his raincoat from the banisters and hanging it on a hook behind the front door. Mummy never ceased to be amazed at the things us children would covet. Brian ignored her and going into the front room he took a square tin Oxo box from the window sill of the bay window and placed the metal lovingly inside together with some other pieces of shrapnel, two hard baked conkers (horse chestnuts) on strings, one of which was a twelver (it had shattered twelve other horse chestnuts held still on their strings by his friends and hit until they broke) and some cigarette cards bundled together with elastic bands.

Daddy saved Brian the cigarette cards from each packet of Player's Weights he smoked, when he didn't roll his own. Carefully laying as thin a sausage of tobacco as he could manage to roll, along the cigarette paper in the machine, he would turn the rollers and finally take it out, licking the edges and putting it in his mouth to light it. The smoke would make me cough.

The pictures on the backs of the cigarette cards were of different infantry soldiers or sometimes the dress robes of Knights of the Garter or Lords. There were about fifty cards to a set and they were of many diverse subjects. I liked to look at the silk robes. I particularly liked one in pale turquoise silk. What a beautiful colour that was. I had never seen clothes like it. Our clothes seemed so dull and drab in comparison. Brian perched on the edge of the window sill and examined a scab on his knee, at the same time kicking the wall with his heels. The scratched wallpaper was a clue to the fact that this was something he often did. I wanted to play with my toys on the ledge but Brian was in the way. Without a thought I bit his bottom and Brian yelled. 'She bit me,' he shouted.

Mummy came into the room, wiping her hands on her apron. 'Shush, you'll wake the baby,' she said crossly, pushing us towards the bathroom. 'I said go and wash your hands,' she added and called after us, 'Don't go using too much water!'

Water, like everything else, was rationed. We were not to use more than 2 inches when we took a bath, which was allowed one night per week. More often than not, we had to use the same water. I know that some people would paint a mark in the bath to make sure they didn't use too much, but Daddy said we didn't have to do that as anyone could see when they had run two inches of water into the bath. It was pretty dirty, with a soap scum on top after we had done with it, as you would imagine. But we just accepted it, like everything else. It was all to help the war effort.

Now Brian and I jostled to see who could get to the basin first, elbowing each other out of the way. Brian won; well, he was bigger and stronger than me. I pretended to cry, but he ignored me so I stopped. Our bathroom was somewhat smaller than the kitchen was, and housed a white enamel bath with claw feet, and a porcelain washbasin attached to the wall, beside which stood a cork-topped wooden linen box for the dirty linen. David would stand on that to reach the sink. There was a small window high up with frosted glass, which you couldn't see out of anyway, unless one balanced on the wooden toilet lid, and opened the window by the curly metal handle. Then you only got the view of Daddy's shed and the coal bunker, so there wasn't much point.

Opposite the washbasin was the toilet with a varnished wooden seat. This had a cistern hanging high on the wall complete with chain and brown varnished wooden handle for flushing. Also high on the wall in the opposite corner was the carved black wooden medicine cabinet where Mummy would keep the asthma pills, Andrews Liver Salts, Beecham's little liver pills and Parish's Food – a red iron tonic which stained our teeth brown. There was also concentrated orange juice, and cod liver oil of malt. Mummy regularly gave us a dessertspoon full of the brown sticky goop. This was available from the baby clinic; we would collect it when Christopher went to be weighed each week. Next to this was the evil-smelling heal-all tube of yellow TCP ointment. Then there was the dreaded Syrup of Figs. This was doled out if we were grumpy, to keep us 'regular'. It was reasoned that, if we were grumpy, our bowels must be irregular. How I hated this medicine. Once when Mummy had given me a spoonful I thought to myself, 'I will show her,' and I refused to swallow it. Of course I tasted the horrible brown syrup for a much longer time so the laugh was on me!

We had a huge airing cupboard next to the toilet. It was built over the hot-water tank. To emerge cold and dripping from the bath and be wrapped in a warm towel taken straight from the airing cupboard, in a drafty bathroom, was the most amazingly comforting thing, and soon stopped your shivering and teeth chattering. 'Tea's on the table,' Sheila called from the living room, 'come and get it!'

We hurriedly finished washing our hands and flicking water at each other. Brian pulled out the rubber plug by its chain; we dried our hands on the damp, threadbare towel that hung from the metal support on the side of the washbasin and returned to the dining room. Sheila had laid the table with a pretty embroidered cloth and a strange assortment of china cups, enamel mugs and some jam jars, there were also some Shippam's fish paste jars. Our china was always getting broken and as we had run out of cups, and there was no money for more, if indeed there had been any available to buy, Brian and I had to drink out of jam jars and paste pots. We didn't mind; it was different.

My other sister, Thelma, arrived home from school at this point. She slammed the front door so that the house shook, and a piece of plaster fell off the wall in the hall, where it had been cracked by the incessant bomb blasts around us. She stamped up the hall in a temper and kicked her shoes off. 'You are late,' Mummy remarked, secretly relieved to see her daughter home safe after the air raids.

'Don't make me wear your shoes again!' Thelma said crossly to Mummy. 'They all laughed at me!'

Thelma's shoes had holes in them. Mummy had cut a piece of cardboard out of the Kellogg's cornflakes packet to put inside and cover the holes. She knew when it was raining that morning that the cardboard wouldn't hold up in the wet so she had given Thelma her own shoes to wear. As Thelma was only eleven Mummy's shoes were somewhat on the large side and rubbed up and down as she walked the half a mile to and from school. Thelma sat down hard on a chair, pulled off her sock, and examined a large red, angry blister on her heel.

She was tall for her age but, like the rest of us, she was on the skinny side, which was not surprising as there never was much food to go around in those days. Unlike Brian and I with our mousy brown hair, Thelma's was a lovely glossy black. Sheila had light brown hair, David's was brown with auburn highlights, and Christopher's fuzz was golden auburn, just like my third sister, Betty. She was fourteen and was always washing her hair; she was so proud of it, and how it would shine!

Betty was at her best friend Peggy's house. Peggy Taylor lived around the corner in Woolwich Road. Betty and Peggy were always chasing the boys. Thelma's hair was wet and it hung down in rats' tails around her pale freckled face so Mummy fetched a towel from the bathroom linen cupboard, draped it over Thelma's head, and at the same time she put her arm around her. 'Don't worry, dear, tomorrow is Saturday and Daddy will be able to mend your shoes,' she said kindly, rubbing Thelma's hair dry.

'Now get your wet things off and come and have some tea.' Thelma's face brightened at the thought of having her own shoes to wear again. She smiled and wrapping the towel around her head, tucked the end in like a turban and ran upstairs to get some dry clothes on. We all sat up to the dining room table with David sitting in the green painted high chair. Sheila was sitting on Mummy's chair by the fire making toast. Having sliced the bread on the round breadboard placed at the corner of the table, she put a slice on a long-handled four-pronged toasting fork, and as each slice was toasted, it was placed on a dinner plate in the hearth. The whole room smelled of warm toast. Rubbing the red marks that were appearing on her legs from the heat, Sheila put the plate on the table. We were having toast and jam for tea. Yummy!

There was no butter but we grabbed the toast and ate hungrily. We loved Mummy's homemade blackberry jelly. We each gulped down a paste pot of weak tea, with a teaspoonful of tinned condensed milk added, to save on the sugar and the milk.

I looked around our living room. The floor had a covering of very old brown linoleum; it had worn through in places and you could see the floorboards beneath. Fresh coal from the coal scuttle had been added to the fire with the brass tongs, as it had been allowed to get low while Sheila made the toast. The once dying embers now burned cheerily in the grate, making dancing shadows on the wall, and bringing warmth back to the room.

Above the fire, on the wall, was an oval mirror with a carved wooden frame. It hung from the picture rail and was turned sideways, filling most of the width of the chimney breast. Beneath the mirror on the mantelshelf was a wooden framed clock. On each end of the mantel stood a barley sugar shaped wooden candlestick, each containing a half-spent candle for using when the electric ran out. The recent mail was propped behind the candlestick on the right. Two small brass dishes completed the picture. One was shaped like an oak leaf, the other a fish. I have them to this day.

Either side of the fireplace stood matching chairs. They were oak-coloured wood with khaki corduroy cushions and could be folded down into beds. Mother's chair was on the right and Father's was on the left. Beside Mother's chair was a tall square carved sewing box on long legs; it was painted black. Lifting the lid revealed a tray for needles and cottons and beneath the tray Mummy kept her darning wools and wooden mushroom for darning the socks. The inside of the workbox was covered with a faded blue, shabby cotton lining. The quilted lining of the lid was used as a pincushion.

In the corner behind Mummy's chair stood a huge 3-foot by 2-foot oak-coloured wooden radio. It was Mother's pride and joy and was polished lovingly. Once when she was sitting there and we were all listening to one of our favourite programmes, our windows were blown in by a bomb blast and a piece of glass flew past Mummy's head embedding itself in the radio. She was mad! I'll bet that old Hitler would have turned pale if he had heard what she said about him! At dinner times and in the evening, we would gather round the radio and listen avidly to the news, and to shows like *ITMA* and *Workers' Playtime*, or maybe *Children's Hour* at five o'clock. There would be *Toy Town* with Larry the Lamb, and cross old Mr Grouser or

Said the Cat to the Dog, with Monty the cat and Peckham the dog. On one occasion, I remember, even the two royal princesses, Princess Elizabeth and Princess Margaret Rose, broadcast to us from Buckingham Palace. After all they had been bombed as well, but the King and Queen refused to leave. If we could take it, then so could they! How we loved them. The programme would always finish with Uncle Mac saying, 'Goodnight children, everywhere.'

Growing up I would listen to *Listen with Mother* when the announcer would attempt to make the children listening take exercise, 'Now stand up and spread out.' I would stand up and stretch out my arms imagining there were other children in the room while Mummy watched with a smile on her face. 'We are trees and we are waving our branches about in the wind.' After the stretching I would sit on the floor and listen to the story, totally lost in what the announcer was saying. 'Are you listening carefully?' the announcer would say. 'Then I will begin.' After *Listen with Mother*, we had to keep quiet while Mummy listened to *Woman's Hour*. Then at four o'clock was *Mrs Dale's Diary*. It always began with Mrs Dale saying, 'I am worried about Jim.'

Behind Daddy's chair was an oak desk, or writing bureau as he would call it. The front lid pulled down to make a writing surface and had a pad of pink blotting paper covered in inkblots, attached with four leather triangles at the corners. There was a stand for pens with an ink bottle either side and behind that were lots of compartments for important papers and letters. One compartment contained red sealing wax and a monogrammed seal. The monogram was A. C. for Arthur Cawley. I was fascinated watching my father melting the wax with a lighted match onto the back of a letter and pressing the brass seal into it.

The bureau had two drawers with hanging brass knobs, which all of us children loved to play with. We would sit sideways on the arm of the chair, flicking them up and down to make them bang against the drawer fronts. Above the desk were three bookshelves holding some of Daddy's prized possessions. The top shelf had his gardening books and the middle shelf had a set of pink encyclopedias, entitled *Peoples of all Nations*. On the bottom shelf was another set of encyclopedias bound in black and gold entitled *The Book of Knowledge*. As Christopher grew up, he took it into his head to learn the titles of the books. He would sit and recite to himself, 'Ab to boa, boa to coo, coo to flo, flo to isis, ita to nav, nav to sca, sca to zwi, Fact Index and Study Outlines.'

It seemed that it was the simple things that kept us amused. Beside these encyclopedias stood my favourite book; it was a thick musical book, and if we had been good, Daddy would wind it up with a very ornate key and it would play wonderful tinkling music. At least I thought so. I would beg him to let us hear it. Next to the desk the huge bay window with the wide sill looked out onto our front garden. My brother Brian and I loved to play with our toys on this sill. I had a cut-out model of the two princesses' Welsh thatched cottage. This cottage had been given to Princess Elizabeth and Princess Margaret Rose as a miniature version of the real thing. I loved my cardboard copy and would spend ages playing with it and arranging the furniture, potted plants and corgi dogs. Mummy tried in vain to keep the window sill tidy.

There were framed photos all around the room hanging from the narrow picture rail. In the corner by the bay window, there was one of Sheila. It was a watercolour that was taken from a photo of her when she was about five years old, plump and smiling, standing with her back to a haystack. Another was of her and Betty when she was a little older. Next to them was one of Thelma and her now-deceased twin Diane Cecelia aged about eighteen months old, dressed in embroidered Hungarian muslin dresses; they were playing with a teddy bear. Thelma's twin sister had died at the age of two from diphtheria.

The twins had been a source of amusement as they were always getting into mischief – even at that young age. Mother would get them ready to go out and sit them in their pram. She only had to turn her back and the twins would begin undressing each other. Another time, when they were dressed in pretty powder-pink coats and bonnets, they were found playing with the coal in the fireplace. Next was a picture of Grandma – my father's mother – looking very fierce, with her hair arranged like a cottage loaf and a very upright back with her stiffly laced bodice. Grandma had died before I was born and I think if I had met her she would have scared me. My grandfather had been a postman and we had a picture of him with his horse-drawn mail cart. He had also been a gardener.

I took another slice of toast and spread it with some of Mummy's dark-crimson bramble jelly. Oh, it was so good!

CHAPTER 2

~⁓

A Bit Close for Comfort

Wendy's parents.

The next morning I awoke. I was sleeping in the front bedroom, which was my parents' bedroom. I had a fold-up bed, in the corner beside a large chest of drawers and Daddy's wardrobe. Beside my parents' bed was a cabinet with a large circular hole in the left-hand door. It had been a radio cabinet at one time and the hole was where the speaker used to be. A built-in cupboard next to it served as Mummy's wardrobe. Next to it was a mahogany table, which my mother used to change Christopher on, and his cot stood beside it.

I remember when Christopher was born, Mummy was lying in bed cuddling him and I was in my small bed in her room. She turned to me and asked, 'What shall we call your new brother?'

Without a pause I said, 'Michael.'

'Well I rather like Christopher,' my mother said.

'Well I like Michael,' I replied.

'How about if we call him Christopher Michael?'

I nodded, 'Yes, Christopher Michael.'

So Christopher Michael he became. I stretched and yawned, then looked across at my mother, who was still asleep in the double bed with Christopher nestled in her arms also sleeping, his thumb firmly in his tiny mouth. I noticed that both their faces were black with the dust that had fallen on them from a gaping hole in the ceiling. A portion of ceiling paper was hanging down over their heads.

We had had an air raid in the night but were all too tired to wake and go to the shelter. A bomb had dropped on the houses opposite – you would have thought that would have awoken us, but I suppose we were just so used to the incessant noise that we just didn't stir on this occasion.

'Mummy, look!' I yelled.

My mother woke and gasped as she looked at Christopher. 'What happened?' she cried. Then she saw the ceiling, and understood.

My father had got up very early and dressed in the dark so as not to wake us; he hadn't seen the gaping hole, or noticed the dust covering his wife and baby. He went downstairs to shave. I raced downstairs to tell him, grabbing tightly to the banister rail as I nearly tumbled in my haste. Then I pushed open the door of the living room as I tried to find him. I gasped in dismay. All the glass in our large bay window was smashed, the curtains were torn and blowing in the wind, and there were shards of glass all over the floor. The blast from the bomb that had brought down the bedroom ceiling upstairs was also responsible for the broken windows. Forgetting my initial reason for finding Daddy, I ran to put my shoes on, and then began to jump up and down on the glass. It made a lovely crunchy noise.

Daddy came into the room to find out what all the noise was about, just as I was getting ready to stamp on an extra-large piece of glass. Wiping the shaving cream from his face with a damp towel, he looked shocked and angry. 'Stop that!' he growled at me. 'Go and get the broom.'

I stopped jumping and looked at his cross expression. 'It wasn't me,' I protested.

The anger disappeared and my father smiled. 'I know,' he said putting his arm around me and giving me a squeeze. 'It's that madman Hitler again.'

We went to the window where the torn curtains flapped in the breeze. Looking out, we saw that across the road from us was a massive pile of smouldering bricks and rubble. It had once been a terrace of four houses and was now reduced to this debris. Daddy looked worried; first Chapel Road at the back of us, and now this, not to mention the aircraft at the end of the road. It was getting just too close for comfort. I stood beside him, my mouth open, transfixed at the devastation before my eyes. Then I suddenly remembered why I had come to find him. I turned to face him. 'Mummy and Christopher are all dirty and the ceiling came down.' The words tumbled out of my mouth and I gasped for breath.

Throwing down the towel, Daddy raced up the stairs two at a time to discover what had happened just as my mother had started to descend with Christopher. 'Are you alright?' he asked, as he took the baby from her. Meanwhile, Sheila began busying herself with the broom, and then Mummy took Christopher into the bathroom to get cleaned up, while I helped Sheila set the table. We sat down for a breakfast of Weetabix spread with a scraping of margarine, as there wasn't enough milk to go round and we had to have some for Christopher. The Weetabix was a bit dry but it tasted good all the same. We gulped jars of water to help it down.

It was Saturday, and half way through the morning the clanking of milk bottles was heard outside and then a rap on the door knocker. The milkman had come for his money.

What a pity he hadn't come earlier so that we could have had milk for breakfast. Mummy picked up her handbag and went to the door. As I stood beside her, staring again at the bomb site across the road, the milkman, standing there in his peaked cap, followed my gaze, beyond his horse and cart. 'That was a bit close for comfort, luv,' he said. Then, nodding towards our damaged front window, he went on, 'I see they got your windows again.' He placed a 1 quart and 1 pint bottle of milk in Mummy's arms.

My mother nodded. 'Thank you very much. Yes, but at least we are all safe and well,' she smiled as she handed him some coins and shut the door, wondering at the same time if her neighbour across the road, in the house second from the end, had somehow managed to escape from the bombing. We heard later that Mrs Mac had managed to hide in the cupboard under the stairs so she had survived, even though the rest of the house was demolished. Though she lost the sight in one eye from a piece of flying debris and from then on always wore a patch over her eye. No one else in the other houses survived that particular bomb blast.

Daddy was going shopping for the leather to repair Thelma's shoes. He loved to repair all our shoes, and took great pride in it. The wooden bench in his small garden shed boasted a metal last with different sized and shaped feet. There was a rack where he kept the sticks of brown and black wax to seal the edges of the leather soles. Recycled Brylcreem jars and Gibbs Dentifrice toothpaste tins of all sizes became containers for his nails. I used to clean my teeth with Gibbs Dentifrice. It came in a tin as a hard block of pink toothpaste and I would wet my brush and rub it on it. Then clean my teeth with the resulting bubbles. It lasted ages. The advertisements in the paper would say, 'Shine your ivory castles.' I would brush until the toothpaste on my brush had disappeared. It never occurred to me to rinse my mouth to get rid of the bubbles, so I suppose I must have swallowed them.

As Daddy shaved he would sing the cobbler's song, 'I cobble all night and cobble all day.' His voice was a lovely deep baritone. He had inherited his lovely singing voice from his Welsh mother. Sometimes he would burst into 'Men of Harlech' singing it in Welsh, or 'We'll keep a welcome in the Hillside':

> We'll keep a welcome in the hillsides. We'll keep a welcome in
> the vales.
> This land you knew, will still be singing, when you come home
> again to Wales.
> This land of song will keep a welcome,
> And with a love that never fails.

My parents had both been keen on amateur dramatics and both had sung on the stage. My father joined a group of men, whom he worked with at the Welgar Shredded Wheat factory in Welwyn Garden City (where my parents used to live when they were first married). The men sang Negro spirituals and they would put black makeup on their faces to look the part, leaving a white space around the eyes and mouth, just like Al Jolson. My father loved listening to Al Jolson singing. He had two of his records, and he could play the wooden bones and the banjo.

As I grew up and listened to him singing, it would make me very proud to think that part of me was Welsh, and I longed to visit Wales and roam the hills and valleys that he told me about. Brian and I cleared the breakfast table, while Mummy attended to the two younger boys. 'Can I come with you, Daddy?' I asked, as I saw him getting ready to go shopping.

'Well, hurry up and get ready then,' he replied, as he stood in front of the fireplace in the living room. Looking at his reflection in the mirror, he combed his dark hair straight back.

Mummy was busy with the baby and David was sitting on his potty in the middle of the living room looking, I thought, somewhat red in the face. Brian had already disappeared to his friend's house. I grabbed the comb from where Daddy had placed it under the clock in the living room (for some reason, this is where it lived). Hurriedly I combed my hair, fastening it back from my face with a hair clip I found in one of the little brass dishes on the mantelpiece, and before I pulled on my coat, I dashed into the bathroom, went to the loo, washed my hands and grabbed a damp flannel, quickly wiping my face.

'A cat's lick and a promise will do,' I thought to myself as I followed Daddy down our two front steps. At the gate he turned to wait for me with a big smile. It was a lovely sunny day and a blackbird was singing in one of our two laburnum trees in the front garden, which were ablaze with bright-yellow racemes drooping like golden waterfalls. Some purple primroses and a few daffodils adorned the flowerbed that encircled the small square lawn in the middle of the garden. It was May and our road boasted an avenue of flowering cherry trees. Their branches were weighed down with the lovely fluffy pink blossoms. I stooped down and picked up a fallen spray, for a moment studying the delicate pale-pink petals and bright green of the leaves. I handed it to my father. As Daddy took it he paused for a moment to gaze on the bomb site across the road. Planks of wood and broken furniture stuck out amongst piles of bricks and rubble, like a gruesome memorial amongst the devastation. He frowned. I didn't want to think about that. I would focus on the flowers instead. 'Look, Daddy, isn't it pretty?' My father looked at the spray and smiled.

'Yes it is,' he agreed, placing it on the hedge as we started off along the road. The sun felt warm on my head. Once more I glanced back at the carnage and again put it out of my mind.

When we reached the end of Pelham Road we turned left into Woolwich Road. I looked across the street to the fighter plane where it had crashed into the ground, tail stuck up in the air. Daddy took no notice of it. Beyond a hedge was the apple orchard belonging to a smallholding where the fruit trees were full of white and pink blossoms. It was Hancocks; a family-owned business, they sold fruit, vegetables and the occasional eggs. Their hens would wander about clucking in and out of your legs looking for scraps whilst you were queuing for vegetables. 'Remind me to get some vegetables on the way home,' said Daddy. I nodded and began to skip. How I loved going out with my Daddy. He was a handsome man his black hair smoothed straight back with Brylcreem. He had a black moustache, which tickled when he kissed me goodnight and thick bushy eyebrows. I gazed up at him as he smiled down at me. I stopped skipping and held his large hand; it was warm and rough and safe. We passed Parkers, the coal merchant's. There was a table outside and

Mrs Parker had put a notice on her garden wall, which read: 'Lettuce 2*d* each.'

'She'll be lucky,' my father said under his breath.

We reached the end of Woolwich Road and came to the Broadway, which was the main shopping area. The clock tower opposite chimed eleven. We turned to look at the buses lined up across the road outside Boots the chemist. The 696 went to Welling, and the 698 went around the clock tower and then past the Congregational church where Thelma, Brian and I went to Sunday School, past the Palace Cinema, and along Mayplace Road East until it turned the corner into Erith Road and finally to the town of Erith. Both were red double-decker trolleybuses attached to overhead wires. We crossed the road and waited for the 696 to take us to the leather shop. There was a commotion. One of the trolleys had come away from the overhead wires and the driver had pulled a long pole from underneath the back of the bus and was frantically trying to catch the electric pole on top of the bus. It was waving around as though it had developed a mind of its own and the driver was getting redder and redder in the face as a small crowd gathered. Suddenly he caught the offending pole and everyone cheered as it was finally attached to the wires.

Smiling, Daddy and I got on the bus together with the other chuckling passengers. These days the smallest thing was enough to make us smile and take our thoughts off what might happen tomorrow. The conductor was whistling happily to himself as he rang the bell twice and we were off! Down the arrow-straight Broadway, which was also called Watling Street and was part of the old Roman road that went from Dover on the south-east coast and eventually led to London.

The conductor, looking very smart in his navy uniform and peaked cap, worked his way along the bus holding onto the seats to steady himself as the bus lurched along – the driver was trying to make up the time lost when the pole left the wire. 'One four penny and a tuppenny half please,' said Daddy, handing the conductor sixpence. The man took two tickets from a wooden ticket carrier in his hand and, putting them into the machine he wore around his neck, punched a hole in each with a ding of his bell, handing them both to me with a grin.

'There you are, luv,' he said. I folded the tickets and put them into a pocket in my dress; I was going to give them to Brian when I got home. I knew I mustn't lose them in case the ticket inspector got on. Brian had a conductor's outfit and we could use them to play buses. We would line up the dining room chairs one behind the other and make believe we were on the bus. Brian would clip my ticket and then hop onto the front chair and pretend to drive the make-believe vehicle. Sometimes we sat David on the front chair so that he could be the driver. He would sit there with his chubby little arms outstretched holding an imaginary driving wheel and making the noise of the bus engine, 'brmm, brmm'.

There was a loud thump as a youth came jumping down the steep stairs from the upper deck, his shoes clattering as he came. He had rung the bell from the top deck and, not waiting until the bus came to the stop, he leaped off backwards to show off. The conductor rang the bell twice. 'Hold very tight please!' he called and we were off again.

Finally we reached Lyon Road and got off by the public library. I loved to go to the library with Mummy too. It was a small green wooden shed-like building with steps up to the front door. Inside they had a children's section with child-size chairs and a small table. I would sit on one of the chairs and look at books of Milly Molly Mandy or Mumpfy the elephant or maybe Orlando the marmalade cat. I just loved books. It would keep me quiet for ages whilst my mother would choose her favourite novels; she was also very fond of reading when she got the chance. I was always allowed to borrow a library book too.

At home Sheila would sometimes sit me on her lap and read to me from my library book or the weekly magazine *Sunny Stories* by Enid Blyton, at the same time sipping a cup of wonderful-smelling Camp Coffee. This was a dark brown liquid, a mixture of coffee and chicory that came in a bottle. She would put a teaspoon of it into a cup adding boiling water and a drop of milk. I remember having a sip of it once and I quite liked it. She would cuddle me as she related the tales of Josie Click and Bun, the little girl and her mouse and rabbit, or the tales of the Five Find Outers and Dog, or maybe Noddy and Big Ears. I would listen enthralled to the stories. Sitting on her lap was such a comforting feeling.

Now as I clung on to Daddy's hand, we crossed over Lyon Road to the leather shop. Climbing the three steep stone steps, we entered the tiny shop. Inside there was a lovely smell of leather. I blinked as we came into the dim shop from the bright sun outside. As my eyes got used to the gloom, Mr Jenner appeared from somewhere in the back, wiping his hands on his brown linen apron. He seemed quite ancient to me with a ruddy complexion, balding head and spectacles on the end of his red nose. 'Hello, Arthur, how're things?' he smiled and rubbed his hands together at the prospect of doing business. Then taking a large jar off the shelf he unscrewed the lid and offered it to me. 'Hello, young Miss, would you like a bullseye?' he asked. I smiled, nodding shyly, and took one of the hard sticky black-and-white-striped, cushion-shaped sweets from the jar he was holding, and popped it into my mouth. It made a lump in my cheek. I loved the peppermint taste of bullseyes. Mr Jenner always had a jar of sweets for his customers' children.

He turned to my father. 'Now what can I get for you, Arthur?' he asked.

'Well,' said Daddy smiling, 'just the usual please, I have more shoes to mend.' Daddy chose his leather and nails, together with a stick of brown wax to seal the edge of the leather soles; they were put into a brown paper bag.

'How's the wife and family?' Mr Jenner enquired, as he folded the top down on the paper bag and placed it on the glass counter.

'Not too bad, but those bombs are getting a bit too close for comfort,' Arthur replied. 'We had one drop just opposite us in the night; it brought the bedroom ceiling paper down, and broke our windows again,' he added frowning. The shopkeeper looked concerned. 'Yes,' my father went on, 'and the noise didn't even wake us!'

'Goodness, well, a lot of people are sending their children away to somewhere a bit safer,' Mr Jenner remarked.

'Yes, I've heard. I have been wondering about sending the children to Canada. Doris has two brothers out there,' my father said thoughtfully, considering his wife's two brothers, Arthur and Reginald Hill, who had emigrated to Alberta during the First World War. 'It might be better for them there,' he said, then looking in my direction, 'but enough of that. Walls have ears.'

I pretended not to hear (though in truth I was barely listening) and gazed out of the open door, watching the traffic and sucking on my bullseye. Mr Jenner grinned and touched his red nose with his finger knowingly.

'Yes, careless talk costs lives,' he whispered. 'Well tata for now,' he added cheerfully, turning to a new customer who had just entered the shop.

'Goodbye to you,' Daddy replied, in his posh voice – he always spoke so beautifully – as he took the bag from his friend; then grabbing my hand he made his way to the door.

We left the dimly lit shop, crossing the street, so that we could walk on the sunny side and began our long walk back up the Broadway. We had decided to walk home as it was so nice, and besides we couldn't afford to ride both ways. Being a Saturday the Broadway was quite busy with shoppers and one or two food stores had long queues outside. This was a sure sign that there was something different to be had. The pale, poorly dressed and skinny people, hoping to pick up something extra to eat, their shopping bags on their arms, waited patiently. Everything was rationed to ensure fair distribution. When a commodity was scarce the government would put the price up to discourage people from buying it. That way it would hopefully last a bit longer. On the other hand it meant that those of us who didn't have two pennies to rub together always went without. Everyone was issued a ration book with coupons, which were torn out by the shopkeeper when you paid for your goods. No ration book, no goods. Just eight ounces of meat per person per week was allowed. With merchant ships being torpedoed in the Atlantic, we just had to make do. After all, the troops must be fed first.

We could be quite creative about finding things to eat and disguising things to look more appetising. Dried and ground up dandelion roots made reasonable coffee. Sheila had managed to get hold of some bright-yellow parachute silk and made herself a blouse. Stockings were in short supply and both Sheila and Betty, as did the other girls of their age, drew a line up the back of their legs to give the appearance of the stocking seam, when they had none to wear.

As we strolled slowly along, enjoying the sunshine, we suddenly heard a loud throbbing noise overhead. When it stopped I was amazed to see everyone suddenly fall to the ground, including Daddy. He grabbed me and pulled me down, putting his arms over my head. I felt the rough pavement against my cheek, grazing it.

I heard a loud whistling noise followed by an almighty explosion. It was a V1 – a flying bomb. Just one of the many kinds of bombs Hitler had devised to try and bully us into submission. Launched from the other side of the English Channel, these unmanned missiles would keep on flying until the power ran out. Then they dropped from the sky causing utter devastation. We were getting used to them now. There was no warning, but we knew once the engine stopped you had better watch out!

The danger had passed and everyone got to his or her feet. Luckily the bomb had dropped far enough away not to affect us too much. I rubbed my scratched face and brushed the dust from my frock. 'Are you alright, Pudden face?' my father joked trying to make light of the situation as he examined my face.

'Yes, thank you, Pie Pace,' I joked back, pushing my hair out of my eyes. Daddy roared with laughter, breaking the tension, and I laughed with him. That was the first time I had called him that, and years later when I was in hospital having an operation for bunions (the result of having to wear ill-fitting shoes passed down from my sisters), he wrote to me and signed himself 'Pie Pace'. It had become my pet name for him.

We continued on, passing the lovely old flint building, Christ Church and the Regal cinema advertising Laurel and Hardy, together with Pathé News. Further on we came to Jennings, the toy and pram shop. They had a beautiful Silver Cross carriage-style pram in the window. The kind the King and Queen had had for the two princesses. Then came Mence Smith, the ironmonger's, then the bank and finally, reaching the clock tower and Woolwich Road, the last leg of the journey, we turned the corner.

Daddy and I were both quiet the rest of the way. He had been thinking about what his friend Bob Jenner had said. I was thinking about the dirt on my dress and what my mother was going to say when she saw it. I later discovered that this was the moment that my father made up his mind that it was just too dangerous – he should send my mother and all us children away. We stopped off at Hancocks, and while I tried to dodge the inquisitive hens running around our feet, Daddy purchased some potatoes, Bramley seedling cooking apples and a cabbage; we finally crossed the road and turned the corner of Pelham Road, which was now looking quite battle-scarred. A small group of people stood chatting and pointing to the mess of rubble opposite our house. Daddy waved to them as we went up our front path.

Mummy was busy making midday dinner and the wonderful aroma of cooking cheese greeted us as we shut the door. We were having macaroni cheese. David was crawling around the floor playing with a small car. Christopher was in his crib smiling and admiring his little hands, holding them out in front of him and turning them this way and that. As usual, Brian was nowhere to be seen.

'Hello,' she said with a smile, then, 'what have you been doing? Look at your dress!'

'It isn't her fault,' said my father. 'We've been dodging flying bombs.'

As if this was a normal thing to do my mother didn't say another word, and after giving us both a hug she took the bag of vegetables from Daddy, and after kissing him on the cheek, she put them away in the cupboard under the larder. As Daddy went into the garden to put the leather in the shed, Mummy turned to me. 'Don't worry about your dress, it will wash out,' she said, kissing the top of my head and stroking my sore cheek. Then, taking me into the bathroom, Mummy gently rubbed some TCP ointment on my face. It smelled awful, and I screwed up my nose. Mummy went back into the kitchen. 'Go and find Brian and tell him his dinner is ready,' she called to me as she took the dish out of the oven, 'he's in the garden.'

I went to find my older brother, calling his name, 'Brian! Where are you?' My brother appeared from behind the shed. He had been amusing himself pulling the thorns off Mr Mepham's roses. The Mephams were our next-door neighbours and their garden was surrounded by wooden trellis; it was a blaze of colour in the summer when it was covered with climbing roses of red, pink and yellow. As some of the roses tumbled over the fence they also brightened our garden. 'Dinner's ready,' I shouted to him and we ran inside to eat. We all gathered around the table in the living room with David in the high chair next to Mummy. As usual we were all starving hungry. Mummy gave Brian and I stale bread to eat with our macaroni; she believed that fresh bread would make us both breathless with our asthma. We didn't care, it tasted good anyway, and when the dish was completely empty, which took no time at all, Mummy went into the kitchen and came back with a large bowl of raspberry jelly, just as though it was someone's birthday! How we enjoyed it – a whole undisturbed meal.

That afternoon, Daddy began work on Thelma's shoes. Singing away to himself in the shed he broke into, 'Old Man river, that old Man river, he must know somethin' but don't say nothin', he just keeps rollin' he keeps on rollin' along. He don't plant taters, he don't plant cotton and them as plants 'em is soon forgotten.' My father's deep baritone voice rang out. How I loved to listen. I think the neighbours rather enjoyed it too as Mr Mepham spent a long time tending his roses next door behind the shed.

Brian was at the end of the garden playing in the dirt. I went to find him. He was pushing a small toy tractor along; as I approached he looked up. 'Let's make mud pies,' I said, joining him and sitting on the ground. It didn't matter as, after all, my dress was dirty already. My brother got to his feet, wiping his dirty hands on his trousers.

'All right, I'll get some water,' he replied happily over his shoulder as he ran down the garden. I knelt on the ground and began searching for cake-sized stones. I found six that were just the right size as Brian returned with the water in a jam jar. Tipping the water into the ground, I began to mix it with a stick to make mud. Then we iced the stones with the mud using our fingers and I picked some dandelions and daisies. I was going to use the petals to decorate the pies. I picked up the stick as I stepped back to admire my work. Brian grabbed the stick from me; now he was getting bored. Seeing a worm, he picked it up and tied it in a knot around the stick; he pulled so hard that the worm broke in half.

I squealed, 'Eeoow!' and started to run. My brother chased me down the garden waving the stick with part of the worm still attached. I dashed indoors and slammed the back door, turning the key. I peered through the window but he was already tired of that game and had gone to talk to Daddy in the shed.

The kitchen was warm and steamy and Mummy was busy making pastry. She had decided to make a pie for next day's pudding. It was important to keep ahead of the chores as one didn't know when the next air raid would happen and disrupt our meals. Her face was floury where she had pushed a lock of hair from her eyes. My mother was wearing a floral pinafore. The straps crossed over at the back and she had tied the ties at the back of her waist in a neat bow. I watched as she deftly rolled the wooden rolling pin back and forward, turning the pastry as she managed to keep the shape even. An oval pie dish filled to the brim with the sliced Bramley cooking apples from Hancocks was sprinkled with sugar and stood waiting for the pastry cover. Carefully lifting the rolled pastry onto the pin Mummy laid it over the apples. As she cut the edges from around the dish, I grabbed a piece of raw pastry with my muddy fingers and popped it in my mouth. It didn't have much flavour but it was something to eat. Mummy tapped my arm. 'Go and wash your hands first; you'll get worms.'

I screwed up my nose and spat the pastry out into the sink. She had just reminded me what I was running from when I burst into the kitchen. But I had no time to wash my hands, as suddenly the siren went and then my father was banging on the back door.

'Open the door,' he shouted. I had forgotten I had turned the key when I was escaping from Brian. Mummy quickly put the pie in the larder, turned off the gas oven, then she ran and fetched Christopher and David while I opened the door. Daddy burst in, grabbed me and pushed me roughly through the door. 'Quick, get in the shelter, and you Brian,' he shouted after my older brother, who was pretending to be a Spitfire, running around the garden with his arms outstretched for wings and making shooting noises with his mouth.

The sound of the anti-aircraft guns could be heard, already booming loudly, and in our eagerness to get somewhere safe, we all ended up trying to climb down the air-raid shelter ladder together. I slipped and landed in a heap at the bottom and Brian landed on top of me. I had hit the side of my head by my eye and it was bleeding. I began to cry. David began to wail in sympathy, and Christopher joined in; he was incensed at being woken so roughly. The guns fired again with a loud boom. We sorted ourselves out, but the noise continued.

'Can't you be more careful?' Mummy asked Brian, upset with having to leave her pie unfinished, and having to disturb the baby. He scowled and began to climb back up the ladder.

'I'm not staying in here to be bombed!' he shouted.

Daddy grabbed his leg. 'You will sit down and be quiet,' he said threateningly, as Mummy found the first-aid box and got out a plaster for my bleeding head. My face was beginning to look as though I had been through a war all by myself. My mother had put Christopher inside the baby gas mask, while she attended to me, and he was going red in the face as he yelled in frustration. Daddy opened up the cover and took him out, cradling him against his shoulder. David sat on the bottom bunk sucking on his thumb and looking bewildered by the confusion around him and Brian climbed onto the top bunk pulling the torn grey army blanket around him.

He was scowling. It always happened when he was having fun. 'I hate Hitler,' he said.

The guns were still booming, and I needed to go to the lavatory. I knew that I would have to hold on until the air raid was over; I was determined that I wasn't going to use the chamber pot under the bottom bunk. I just hoped that I could wait!

Luckily for me the raid was soon over and the 'all clear' sounded. This time the bombers had passed over us without discharging their bombs. They were on their way to the Woolwich dockyards to create mayhem there. I blinked as we came up from the shelter and out into the sunshine. Brian pointed to a barrage balloon floating above us – it seemed huge and was tethered by a rope to an army vehicle. The army used these devices to somehow deter the enemy planes. To us, there was something magical and endearing about them as though they could protect us.

Mummy went back to the kitchen to finish her apple pie, after once more putting the babies down for a nap. Thank goodness she hadn't yet put the pie in the oven. She would have been so cross if it had burned. You just couldn't waste any food. We needed every scrap.

Brian again joined our father in the shed and watched as he put Thelma's shoe onto his cobbler's last, cut a piece of leather to match the size of the sole and hammered small nails neatly around the perimeter. He then trimmed the edges so that they were flush with the edge of the sole and finally, lighting a scrap of candle, he melted the stick of wax in the flame and ran it around the edges to seal them. Brian and I were fascinated as he worked. Daddy smiled and hummed to himself as he did the transforming repair. The shoes looked just like new again.

That evening Daddy presented Thelma with her newly repaired shoes. As usual he had polished them until you could almost see your face in them. He loved polishing our shoes. Every evening he sat in the kitchen cleaning the shoes, as he had done when he was in the army during the 1914–1918 war, and singing to himself. Although in those days it was spit and polish he used, but now we had Cherry Blossom Boot Polish. Thelma was so pleased to have her shoes back and she smiled from ear to ear, giving him a big hug.

Daddy never told us much about his time as a sergeant in the army during the First World War. Except that he spent some time in the trenches in France. Once, he said, he was hiding out in a deserted house from the Germans: 'It must have been haunted because I was in this room when I heard loud footsteps walking in the corridor outside and when I looked there was no one there!' How unfair it seemed that my parents had to endure two wars during their lifetimes. But how strong it had made them; it seemed to me that they could face anything. Daddy kept his medals locked away in his desk drawer together with his bayonet. He never told us what the medals were for and we never discovered it.

After tea, Mummy was sitting in her chair by the radio darning socks. She took one of Daddy's socks out of her sewing cabinet and placing her wooden mushroom inside it, right beneath the hole. She took a double thread of wool, working a small running stitch around the hole and then she sewed rows of wool across the opening. She then deftly wove the remaining length of wool in and out, over and under the stretched rows until the hole had disappeared and in its place was a neat darn.

Daddy brought up the subject of evacuation. 'I was talking to Bob Jenner in the leather shop this morning,' he began. 'He was saying that it might be a good idea if the children were evacuated away from the air raids.' Mummy was just about to start on yet another hole in the sock she was holding. The wooden mushroom fell into her lap, the needle still poised in her hand, as her jaw dropped.

'What, on their own, without us?' she asked with a catch in her voice. 'How?'

'Well, lots of people are sending their children to safety,' Daddy continued. 'I believe it's done through the schools. I was thinking that maybe they might go and stay with your brothers in Canada.'

'But that is such a long way for them to go,' Doris argued, tears welling up in her eyes at the thought of being separated from her children, not knowing what was happening to them and, worse, the children not knowing what was happening to their parents. Besides, it was ages since she had heard from either of her brothers. She wasn't sure she would like her family to be so far away from home. How would they keep in touch? On the other hand things were not very rosy living so close to London. Doris gazed out of the window at the bomb site across the road.

Meanwhile Thelma, Brian and I sat silently listening. My eyes grew wide as I looked from my mother to Thelma. She had a funny sort of scared look on her face. While my brother's face was pale as he stared into the fireplace. I was not sure I liked the sound of this. I didn't want things to change. I began to feel frightened and as the familiar tightness started in my chest I began to wheeze. 'Brian, go and get the asthma tablets,' my mother said, as she put her arm around my shoulders.

She kept a small bottle of ephedrine hydrochloride tucked handily just inside the medicine cabinet in the bathroom; the pills were used to help us to breathe. Brian got the tablets and handed the bottle to Mummy. She decided that I would be better in bed so helped me up the stairs and put on my pyjamas. I climbed slowly into bed. I was now devoid of energy. I had to have three pillows, as I couldn't breathe if I lay down. The pillows would support my shoulders and head. As I lay there propped up, the tablets started to take effect. I felt as though my head was swelling, and my hands felt as though they had grown to an enormous size. It was a strange feeling; the ephedrine was taking effect. In a moment I was fast asleep.

The next day being Sunday we had to go to Sunday school. It was a good time for Daddy and Mummy to have some peace from us, so Thelma, Brian and I were dressed in our best clothes with our shoes shining and packed off to the Congregational church at the end of Chapel Road.

In the church hall we were divided into different groups according to our age. This particular Sunday we had a visit from a missionary. Her name was Gladys Aylward and she told us all about her missionary work in China. We sang hymns and cut out pictures to stick onto a poster we were making for the wall. I quite enjoyed going to Sunday school, singing the hymns and listening to the stories of Jesus:

> Tell me the stories of Jesus,
> I long to hear,
> Things I would ask Him to tell me
> If He were here.
> Scenes by the wayside, tales of the sea.
> Stories of Jesus, tell them to me.

Although I think my favourite time was the Christmas party, when I got to see Father Christmas face to face and receive a gift, and my second favourite was harvest festival when Mummy would buy some apples and polish them until they shone so that we could put them in front of the altar, together with all the other fruits and vegetables and some cleverly shaped loaves of bread looking like sheaves of wheat. We would sing:

We plough the fields and scatter the good seed on the land

For it is fed and watered by God's almighty hand.

He sends the snow in winter, the warmth to swell the grain,

The breezes and the sunshine,

And soft refreshing rain.

All good gifts around us are sent from Heaven above,

So thank the Lord, Oh thank the Lord

For all his love.

Nothing more was mentioned about us going away, so assuming it was not going to happen, I promptly forgot about it. The following Monday, as I got ready for school, I decided that my toys would be safer if I were to put them in the shelter. Just in case our house was bombed. So I grabbed my favourites, ran downstairs to the shelter and placed them on my bunk.

We didn't get a bombing raid that day, thank goodness, and in the afternoon when I returned from school I was annoyed to discover that my toys were back in the house. Mummy had been tidying up. Placing my hands on my hips, I confronted her. 'Why did you put my toys back in the house?' I demanded. 'They might have got bombed,' I added crossly.

'Oh,' replied Mummy, her hands on her hips, copying my pose, 'and what about your brothers and me being bombed?'

I looked at her in horror. That idea had not occurred to me and I became very thoughtful and rather frightened. I put my arms round her waist and held on tightly. Christopher had been sleeping with his thumb in his mouth, curled up under his knitted baby blanket on Mummy's chair by the fire. Our voices woke him and he started to stir and began to whimper. I went over to him, picked him up and rocked him in my arms as I sat with him on the chair and made up a song to soothe him.

Mummy's little baby,
Mummy's little boy,
Mummy's little baby,
Mummy's pride and joy.

We all love our baby,
Yes we love him too,
We all love our baby,
Inky Pinky Poo!

I blew a raspberry into his warm neck and tickled his toes; he began to chuckle. I gave him a hug and put him on the floor where he lay kicking his feet, looking at me and smiling. He was such an adorable and happy baby. I loved him very much.

In the following days and weeks, we got more bad news about Hitler's advances across Europe. We also heard the news about a passenger ship, *The City of Bonares*. It had been carrying many children to Canada and hopefully safety, when it was torpedoed in the middle of the Atlantic. All but a handful of children went down with the ship. The remaining survivors managed to make it to the lifeboats and were floating on the ocean for several days before being picked up cold, wet and half starved. So Daddy changed his mind; it seemed that wherever you went there was danger these days. What to do for the best? He had to be sure to make the right decision. So finally it was decided that Thelma, Brian and I would go away together, to a safer place in England with our schools. We were not told where we were going; everything had to be a secret. You never knew who was listening; it might be the 'enemy within', whatever that was.

CHAPTER 3

Tears & Goodbyes

We didn't have a great deal of time to get things ready for going away, not that we had much to get ready – all we were allowed to take was one change of clothes, which was about all we had anyway. The day dawned grey with a soft drizzle, which soaked us to the skin and made us shiver. Mummy had packed our belongings in two carrier bags. We didn't possess much in the way of clothes and we had been told to travel light. Thelma carried a bag that had a few clothes for her and some for me. Brian carried his own. We wore our coats, hats and gloves. I had a knitted woolly bonnet that Mummy had made for me, and my best coat (well, it was my only coat), which was brown tweed with a brown velvet collar. Mummy had found it at the WVS used clothing shop, up near the clock tower in the Broadway. She had been delighted and picked it up just as another woman was about to grab it. The woman had glared at Mummy but my mother was so pleased to see something of decent quality that she smiled back at the woman and held on to it.

I had two jumpers on underneath my coat to save me carrying them. It was a little tight but good enough to 'do me a turn'. Brian had his school cap and his gabardine raincoat (another find from the clothing shop). Thelma wore her brown school beret and gymslip, with her brown blazer jacket. She wore her belted brown raincoat over the top. Our Mickey Mouse gas masks were in their cardboard boxes around our necks and we each had a luggage label pinned to our coats with our name and address and school on, in case we should get lost.

We had got up early that morning to make sure that we didn't miss the bus, and as we hugged and kissed goodbye to Daddy, I noticed that his eyes looked wet.

'Bye-bye, Daddy!' we said in chorus.

'Bye-bye, look after yourselves,' he said gruffly.

Mummy put Christopher, wearing his knitted bobble hat, in the pram and strapped David, in his balaclava hat, onto a small baby chair on top. We trundled our way along the path from Woolwich Road, which divided the two senior school playing fields, half a mile to Church Road school. Thelma had a fixed expression with her lips jammed tightly together. Brian and I dragged our feet; we were really not looking forward to this. Soon we joined other families all going in the same direction. What a sorry sight it was to see lines of small young children leaving home and their families for the first time. When we reached the school, we could see rows of red London buses waiting to take us to the station. There were lots of tears, as one would imagine. But many of the children just looked blank and shell-shocked. Some mothers at the last moment were unable to let their child go and grabbed them back as they alighted the bus.

Thelma, Brian and I said goodbye to Mummy and kissed David and Christopher, giving them all a hug. David began to grizzle seeing us go, in keeping with all the other tears that were flowing that day. 'Now Thelma, you make sure you take good care of them,' Mummy said, sniffing. 'You are in charge now,' she said with a break in her voice. Opening her handbag she took out the bottle of asthma tablets, handing them to Thelma, who put them carefully into her bag.

I looked at my mother; her face was red and tears were falling down her cheeks. She blew her nose on a tiny lace-edged hanky as she waved goodbye to us. I climbed onto the bus with Brian and Thelma close behind. Thelma and I sat together and Brian sat in front of us. As the bus began to move away from the kerb, Thelma turned her face to the window to catch the last sight of Mummy. When she turned back, her face was wet. I noticed Brian wiping his nose on his sleeve. The sky became darker as it began to rain harder. I blinked back my tears; it seemed as if the whole world was crying. I felt so sad.

The journey to the station didn't take long and as the bus stopped a large lady in green WVS uniform, her brown curls peeping out from her hat, stood holding a clipboard. As she herded us off the bus, her best official voice boomed out with urgency. 'Come along there all of you! Don't dawdle, we have to hurry, the train is waiting!' Thelma took hold of my hand and stood close to Brian. We shuffled along, following the other children onto the train, and then, finding a carriage with a table and seats either side, we sat down together. Well, this was better. I couldn't remember having gone on a train before, so this was an adventure. I looked at Brian and he smiled at me, a watery smile. Then, taking the 'Beano' comic out of his bag, he spread it out on the table to read. I half glanced at 'Lord Snooty and his friends' then turned and looked out of the window. The train gave an enormous chuff and the guard blew his whistle as we began to steam out of the station. The train gathered speed as I gazed at the gardens of the houses rushing by, each one complete with the government issue of the Anderson shelter. Then, every so often, I saw complete gaps in the rows, or the shells of buildings and furniture teetering on the edge of now non-existent floors. Gaping holes surrounded by piles of bricks and rubble, and blocked roads with makeshift fences around huge bomb craters to keep the children from playing there.

The engine driver sounded the whistle as we rushed through a long tunnel. The piercing whistle made me jump and I turned to Thelma as she squeezed my arm to attract my attention. Another lady in WVS uniform was handing out Ovaltine sweets. This lady was much slimmer than the other one; she looked kind and smiled at us as she handed us the sweets. I smiled back shyly. We took them and bit into them hungrily – they tasted very good. It seemed a long time since our breakfast wheat flakes.

On and on the train went, never stopping as it was full and they had to make sure that no children would try to get off and go back home before they had reached their destination. Soon it became very noisy with youngsters, releasing their pent-up feelings, chasing their newfound friends. The children ran backwards and forwards along the corridors and some were jumping all over the seats. Brian and I joined in the fun while Thelma sat sedately watching us, making sure we didn't go too far.

The large lady appeared and the sound stopped in a moment as all of the children melted away into their places. She looked very fierce. I needed the lavatory. Thelma took my hand and we made our way to the end of the carriage, lurching from side to side with the motion of the train. Reaching the toilets, we squeezed ourselves into the tiny cubicle. It felt very strange going to the toilet while it kept moving. We washed our hands and Thelma cupped her hand under the cold-water tap and took a drink; I copied her, as I was thirsty too.

We watched the sun go down as on and on we travelled. Now it was dark and we could see our reflections in the windows of the carriage. Finally we reached our destination and as the train puffed into the station we waited patiently until it came to a halt before, clutching our belongings, we jumped down to the darkened platform. There wasn't a light anywhere, and as we stumbled along the platform blindly, we had no idea where we were as a large sign on the station was painted out, but we later learned that we were in Burnley. We had arrived in Lancashire in the north of England.

As we formed a long crocodile, under the direction of the WVS ladies, each child, complete with luggage label and gas mask slung on their back, and a pitiful array of belongings, had to hold hands with a partner as we were marched in twos out of the station and along the street until we reached a school. Then, hurriedly the volunteer helpers ushered us into a large hall with camp beds as far as I could see from wall to wall. Huge blackout blinds covered the large windows. The boys were then all separated from the girls and both Thelma and I became very worried as we saw Brian look back briefly as he disappeared through a door with the other boys. It wouldn't do to have boys and girls all sleeping in the same room. 'Now don't you worry,' shouted the big lady with the loud voice, eyeing the looks on our faces, 'you will see each other in the morning.' Thelma and I found the girls' cloakrooms and when we returned we were shown to two adjoining folding camp beds. We didn't want to get undressed in this huge place in front of everyone, so we got on the bunks fully clothed and pulled the scratchy blankets up under our chins.

A small girl wearing a cotton frock and a blue knitted cardigan was in the next bed to mine. I had noticed her on her own earlier. I smiled at her shyly but she glared back at me. 'Wot you looking at?' she asked rudely. As she was travelling alone, her defensive strategy was to be ready to fight anyone who crossed her.

'Nothing,' I whispered and turned over to face Thelma.

Why did she have to be so mean? I didn't like it here. I was cold, I wanted my Mummy and why had Brian had to go? Things were starting to get scary again. Everything was strange and I didn't like it. I began to wheeze as my chest started to tighten through having to lie down. Thelma leaned over and gave me her pillow so that I was propped up. I must have been tired because I don't remember any more until I awoke with a jump. It was early in the morning and not yet light. The large lady was ringing a hand bell as she switched on the bright lights. I opened my eyes and blinked. 'Come along, come along, all of you, you must get up now!' she bellowed, her huge chest heaving up and down as she shouted.

The rude girl in the next bed had already got up and was pulling her blanket up over the bed but not before I noticed a large yellow stain on her sheet. She had wet the bed and judging by the strong smell of ammonia in the hall she wasn't the only one. I turned and couldn't see Thelma anywhere. I started to panic. Then I breathed a sigh of relief as I saw her coming through the far door with Brian. As I had been asleep when she awoke, Thelma hadn't wanted to disturb me, but remembering that Mummy had told her to look after us, she had gone to find Brian. As they made their way between the rows of beds I noticed the telltale sign of Brian having an asthma attack. His shoulders were hunched and he was walking slowly as he struggled to breathe. He sat down on my bed his hands gripping the sides and his shoulders hunched up as he wheezed helplessly.

It was time for a medical examination by a doctor and nurse to check on our health before we were to be passed over to our new foster parents. We were made to line up along the wall leading to the medical room. Once Thelma, Brian and I went together through the closed door, the doctor listened to our chests and the nurse probed our hair for lice with two glass rods. Brian sat down and was given some water and an ephedrine asthma tablet from the bottle Thelma was guarding with her life. 'They're fine, next!' said the doctor dismissing us.

We were then made to go into the next, much larger room, which was teeming with grown-ups, all looking to find the evacuees who would be assigned to them. I looked around and noticed some children were already leaving with their new foster parents. Some woman came up to me. She wore bright-red lipstick and a funny-shaped flowerpot hat with a tall feather in it on her peroxide-blonde hair. She was also wearing a dead fox draped around her shoulders. Having its tail in its mouth helped it hold onto her shoulders. How strange! She bent down and looked me over and grabbed my hand as I frowned and stared back at her, my large eyes mesmerised by the dead fox's face. 'You can coom and live with me,' she announced brightly in a la-de-da voice with a strange accent. 'I have a playpen you can play in.'

I scowled at her. I was five! Couldn't she see I wasn't a baby? I didn't need a playpen. She turned as the WVS lady came up behind her. 'No, you can't have her; these three children have to go together.' She indicated Brian and Thelma beside me. She smiled at me kindly as I breathed a sigh of relief. I didn't like that woman. Shrugging her shoulders, she turned away tugging on the dead fox, and moved on to the next child. More people came and peered down at us, then turned away. I was beginning to feel rather rejected; it was a bit like being for sale in a market, with the prettiest, good-looking children being more desirable than us. The crowded room slowly emptied as children were finally chosen and taken off by their new 'families'. Some seemed happy to go, but others dragged their feet and, wearing worried expressions, followed dejectedly behind their new 'family'. Thelma put her arm around Brian's shoulder and clasped my hand tightly; there was a determined look on her face. Nobody was going to separate her from her little sister and brother!

I looked up as two little old ladies stood before us. They both wore hats. One lady was thin and the other one was plump. They had nice smiling faces, I decided as I looked up at them hopefully. Would they want us? I wondered. They whispered something to the lady in charge. She shook her head slowly.

An older couple stood next to the old ladies and peered at Brian. It turned out that the two ladies could not take three children. 'We joost doon't have the room,' the plump one said, with that strange accent. It was finally decided that the older couple would take Brian to live with them, whilst Thelma and I could go with the two ladies. Thelma looked as though she was about to burst into tears.

'But I have to take care of them,' she said through watery eyes and with a catch in her voice. The plump lady took her hand gently.

'Doon't you worry yersel, lass,' she said kindly in her funny accent, 'yer can see him anytime yer like, he won't be very far away, joost int' next toon.'

So it was decided and Thelma and I said goodbye and hugged Brian. We then followed the two ladies out of the school, while Brian, with a worried backward glance but at the same time trying to look nonchalant, his breathing now easier, disappeared with the other couple.

'Well noo,' said the plump one. 'You can call me Aunty Dora, and this is Aunty Adelia,' she said pointing to her friend, who smiled in agreement.

As we walked across the school playground, I prodded my sister and in a hushed voice said, 'Don't they talk funny?'

Thelma nodded and held my hand tightly. She bent down and whispered in my ear. 'Shoosh they will hear you!' she said.

We had to catch a bus, and as the sun came up we saw a green double-decker waiting at the bus stop. Thelma and I stepped up on to it, with the two ladies close behind. I sat next to Thelma whilst the two ladies sat in the seat across the aisle from us. A few more people got on and then we were off, rattling along the cobbled streets.

I peered around Thelma and examined the two women. They both wore long skirts to their ankles and navy felt hats with large shiny hatpins to hold them in place. Aunty Adelia limped and walked with a stick as she had a club foot; they both smelled strongly of lavender. Thelma and I were very quiet; I was wondering how Brian was getting on. Thelma would turn and smile shyly at the two old ladies from time to time, as they sat chatting among themselves, but she said nothing, while I just scowled. We looked out of the window. I was hungry. My tummy felt emptier than usual and it was making gurgling noises. Having had no breakfast, I hoped that there might be some bread and dripping for us when we reached the house. It seemed an age since we had had any sort of meal, which in fact it was. We were travelling along the narrow streets now, passing rows and rows of terraced houses all exactly alike. I noticed there didn't seem to be any bomb sites though. The bus left the town behind and we were going along a country road and finally came to another town. This town was called Padiham. I learned later that Brian had gone to live in Burnley, the town we had left behind, with Major and Mrs Hargreaves. It was true – it wasn't that far away.

When we came to get off the bus the sun had come out. I noticed a funny smoky smell, a bit like wet coal. The two Aunts carried our small bag. The streets were cobbled with huge round stones, and I found it difficult to walk on them, trying to avoid the puddles, my small feet slipping on the wet surface. Finally, we arrived in Canning Street; it was a long street of terraced houses all looking exactly alike. The front steps of the houses shone white in the sunlight. Later I learned how proud the northern women were of their front step. It had to be scrubbed every day and rubbed with some hard white brick that kept it bright and white.

Dora Cronshaw and Adelia Curtis had lived in this house for many years and had never married. They had been friends since they were girls when Dora took it on herself to look after Adelia and protect her from the unkindness of school 'friends' who would sometimes poke fun at her club foot and the way she walked.

Now Aunty Dora put down Thelma's bag on her gleaming step and unlocked the door of the end house, number 19. She beckoned us in and we found ourselves in the front room with a large sofa, a small table and an oak sideboard. It was spotless and everything was polished till it shone. A pristine white lace curtain covered the window and there were two china dogs on the window sill. An embroidered fire screen stood in front of the empty fireplace, which had two brass dogs beside it. The small oak table was dressed with a crocheted lace centrepiece and topped with a large green-leaved potted plant. There was a strong smell of lavender and beeswax.

We were ushered through to the parlour where a fire was barely burning in the grate with a metal guard in front of it to protect the carpet from any sparks. Two armchairs stood either side of the fireplace. They both had crocheted chair backs and antimacassars. The table in the centre of the room was set with three places for breakfast. Dora and Adelia had only planned to take in one child, but when they saw us they changed their minds. Adelia took off her hat after first removing a long hatpin. She then removed the guard and gave the fire a poke with a long metal poker, which was then returned to its hook. She stepped back as the fire burst into life with a shower of sparks and a loud crackle, instantly appearing to warm the room with bright orange flames.

Aunty Dora removed her pearl-tipped hatpin and took off her hat. She noticed that I was hopping from one foot to the other. 'Well, I expect you will be wanting the lavatory,' she said smiling, 'come with me.' Aunt Dora took my hand, and with Thelma following, we were led through the dimly lit scullery and out of the back door to a walled yard. In one corner stood a tiny brick building. It had a wooden door that didn't quite reach the ground. An outside lavatory! That was strange! I had never seen that before. I went in, shutting the door behind me and pushing the metal bolt. While sitting on the polished wooden seat, I noticed on the back of the door was a nail from which hung neatly cut squares of newspaper threaded through with string, for toilet paper. I finished quickly as I could see a large spider spinning a web in the corner by the door. The newspaper felt rough to my tender skin and the newsprint came off on my fingers. I waited for Thelma as Aunty Dora had returned to the scullery, and I started to giggle. This was funny. I was starting to feel a little better; maybe it wouldn't be so bad staying here after all. I could see Thelma's shoes beneath the door, and as I looked around the paved yard, there was not a blade of grass to be seen, or a flower. I noticed a large grey tin bath hanging on the wall. On the other side stood a mangle for squeezing water out of the laundry. It was just like ours at home!

Thelma and I returned to the house, and as we went through the kitchen we found Aunty Adelia busy frying bacon. My mouth began to water with the wonderful aroma and the sound of the sizzling bacon. 'Coom and wash your hands,' she said pointing to the old stone sink and the towel hanging on a hook. 'I expect you are hoongry,' she added. We were treated to a breakfast fit for a King. There was bacon, egg and fried bread. It was just amazing to have all three. To add to it all, Aunty Adelia poured the bacon fat onto our plates. 'You can soak it oop with t'bread,' Adelia told us. I learned later that the Aunts had saved their ration of bacon so that we could have a good breakfast on our arrival. They sat and watched us eat with broad smiles on their faces. They told us that they kept hens and a cockerel on a small piece of land that they owned across the road from their house to provide them with eggs – just like we did at home. The table was set with matching china; little pale-yellow square plates, with a picture of a cottage surrounded with flowers on each one. It was a long time since we had seen matching china. Thelma and I ate hungrily. After all, it was the first meal we had had since we left home. We were also given tea in pretty matching cups and saucers. Aunt Adelia removed a yellow knitted cosy before she poured the tea from the pot, which was shaped like a cottage with a thatched roof. What a treat! Thelma and I were fascinated by it all.

We finished the meal, using our bread to wipe up the extra bacon fat poured onto our plates. We ate every scrap, then Aunty Adelia asked us if we would like to see our room. We were shown to a brown-carpeted staircase that was between the front and back rooms. At the top of the stairs were two bedrooms. Thelma and I would be in the one on the right. Inside, the room was decorated with faded pink floral wallpaper. There we found a double bed complete with a pink satin eiderdown, a chest of drawers and a built-in cupboard for a wardrobe. We put our bag on the bed and went to look out of the window. We pulled aside the net curtains and down below we could see the paved yard with the outside privy. As far as we could see there were similar yards, all as alike as peas in a pod.

Thelma pointed to the metal tub hanging on the wall, turning to Aunt Adelia. 'Is that the bath?' she asked with surprise. As there didn't appear to be a bathroom indoors, it seemed an obvious assumption. Aunt Adelia followed her gaze.

'Aye, that's reet,' she replied, 'we bring it into the scullery and bathe in the warm.' Then seeing Thelma's face she went on, 'Ye'll get used to it, loove, and if you need to go to the lavvy in the night, you don't have to go outside. There is a chamber pot under your bed,' she continued, lifting up the coverlet and bringing out a huge floral chamber pot with a large handle. Then looking at my white face she went on, 'Why don't you both have a nap? You must be tired.' Thelma nodded. 'You can put your clothes in the chest of drawers and the cupboard when you wake oop,' Adelia added, placing our bags on the floor as she turned to leave.

Slipping off our shoes, we both climbed onto the soft bed and curled up under the large pink eiderdown. Thelma put her arm around me and, at the same time, she wiped away a tear that had somehow escaped from my eye and run down my cheek. Mummy and Daddy seemed so far away now. When would we see them again?

CHAPTER 4

Life in Lancashire

Aunty Adelia.

I awoke to find the sun streaming through the window. Thelma was already up and brushing her long hair. I rubbed my eyes and yawned, and then I realised where I was and quickly jumped out of the bed as Aunty Dora gently tapped on the door and came into the room. 'Oh, you are oop,' she said smiling, as she drew back the curtains. 'I thought I heard you. Did you have a nice nap?' I nodded. 'Well, you coom down now and we will go for a walk, the sun is oot,' she added. Aunty Adelia was sitting by the fire knitting. She looked up and smiled as we went in. 'Thowt we'd go for a walk and show t'girls what's what,' Aunt Dora said brightly.

'Reet then,' replied Adelia, putting down her knitting pins.

We put on our hats and coats, and the Aunts led us out of the front door and across the street. The sun was shining on the wet pavement. As I paused to splash in a puddle, Thelma turned to wait for me and then took my hand as I smiled at her. The nap had done us both good; we were feeling almost human. There was still that funny smell of wet coal I had noticed before, though the cobblestones were dry now. A wire fence surrounded the small piece of grassy meadow opposite the house that was owned by the

Aunts. The rickety gate in the fence squeaked as Aunt Dora opened it, she beckoned us to follow her. Five or six brown hens were pecking at the ground near the fence; they rushed over expectantly as we entered. I noticed a small wooden shed for the hens to nest in and for cover through the night. 'It's like their own little house,' Thelma observed.

Aunt Dora opened the door of the shed to reveal several nesting boxes. Two large brown eggs lay in the straw in one of them. 'Remind me to pick them oop when we come back,' she said cheerfully. 'The hens really are laying very well at the moment, thank goodness,' she said, shutting the door again and fastening the lock.

'See here,' Dora smiled, 'over there is the cockerel. Don't get too close to him or he might peck you,' she added, pointing to the far side of the meadow. 'He rules the roost.' A cockerel with a beautiful red comb and wonderful curly tail feathers strutted around and several brown, black and white hens were following him and pecking at the ground around the shed, happily clucking and looking for worms. One large brown hen began a tug-o-war with an especially fat worm. As she won the battle, the hen gobbled it down and I shivered remembering the worm my brother had tied around a stick. How long ago that seemed now.

'We keep hens at home too,' observed Thelma, 'but we don't have a cockerel.'

'Then you will know how to feed them,' remarked Dora, as she took some grain from a bowl she was carrying and sprinkled it on the ground in front of her. 'We are hoping to get some chicks from these. Here coopy, coopy, coopy,' she called and they all came running. She emptied the bowl and left it by the gate.

Thelma and I smiled and nodded in agreement as we followed the Aunts out of the hen enclosure, into the grassy meadow, which sloped down to a small stream. We walked amongst the buttercups and daisies and I stooped down and picked a buttercup. Holding it under my chin so that the golden petals reflected on me, I walked up to Thelma. 'Do I like butter?' I asked her.

'Coom on,' called Dora as she made her way towards the stream, 'now we will show you where we buy our gravy.' How odd! We had never bought gravy before. Mummy always made ours herself with Oxo and flour or sometimes Bisto. I pictured her standing at the stove in our kitchen wearing her large flowered coverall apron and stirring the gravy with her wooden spoon, mixed with the meat juices in the pan; I remembered how good it smelled. I began to feel a little homesick. I wondered if she was missing us as much as I was missing her and Daddy.

We strolled along the muddy footpath, stepping round a huge puddle and over the small wooden bridge that crossed the stream, as it tumbled noisily over the small rocks and boulders. I tossed the buttercup into the water and watched it float away. We wandered slowly along another footpath until we came to yet another cobbled street and at the end was the shop. It stood on the corner, a small establishment that appeared to sell just about everything. The sign over the door read 'Winterbothams Grocer'. Thelma recalled something Daddy had told her: 'Daddy says Mr Winterbotham is a cold stern man,' she said, and we all laughed at the joke.

We went inside. A poster on the wall advertising Bisto showed the two Bisto kids in their familiar berets, their noses up sniffing the air. There were rows of large glass bottles containing different sweets: bullseyes, sherbet lemons, twirly sticks of barley sugar and jelly babies. Along the front of the counter was a row of square tins with glass tops. They were filled with biscuits of all kinds. You could also buy a bag of broken biscuits, for half price. But of course you had to have the ration coupons. 'Reet,' said Dora, 'on Tuesdays we will be having meat pies for dinner and you must take the jug and coom and buy the gravy to go with them,' she said to me. A formidable woman behind the counter smiled at us as Aunty Dora introduced us to her.

'These are our two evacuees,' and nodding at me, 'Wendy will be coming to get our gravy for us on Tuesdays,' she added.

Mrs Winterbotham opened the box of biscuits and taking out two she handed one each to Thelma and me. 'I am happy to meet you both,' she said with a smile. We took the biscuits and thanked her politely.

'I have never bought gravy before,' I remarked. 'Will it be hot?'

'No, it will be cold but yer Aunty will heat it up int saucepan when you get it home.'

Sure enough, Tuesday came and I found myself carrying a large white china jug, tripping over the little wooden bridge and going to the corner shop to buy three pence worth of gravy. I then had to carry the jug with the gravy carefully back home over the wooden bridge and up the incline through the meadow without spilling a drop. It seemed that it was special gravy from the meat used to make the meat pies and it had a special flavour. We had mashed potatoes and peas with the meat pies and gravy; it tasted very good!

Tuesdays became my favourite day as I looked forward to the pies and gravy. But I also became very happy when Friday came as when I entered the front door I could smell the wonderful aroma of Lancashire teacakes baking. Eating them, split with a dab of margarine, and pulling out the currants, must have been close to heaven! Aunt Adelia loved to bake.

'Where is your air-raid shelter?' I asked her one day. I had been wondering this for a while.

'We doon't have one, loov,' she replied.

'But where do you go when the bombs drop?' I asked again.

'They doon't drop here,' said Dora. 'That's why you were sent here, to get away from them,' she added kindly.

I thought about this for a while. 'Why don't they come here?' I enquired. The Aunts exchanged looks, not knowing what to say. It didn't make sense to me. After all, bombs had been dropping ever since I could remember. It was a natural part of everyday living. It was certainly going to be quiet around here without the crazy rushing to the shelter having dropped whatever you were in the middle of doing. How was I going to get used to this? It was strange not to have to keep getting up in the middle of the night or to have to go to the shelter while we were eating, or worse, on the lavvy! Spending the rest of the night or day on a cold, damp, hard bunk, with all the noise and mayhem going on outside, until the 'all clear' went.

The Aunts knew that we must continue our education and so they managed to find a place for me in the infants' school nearby and a place for Thelma in the senior school, which was on the first floor of the same building. I wasn't sure that I wanted to go to this strange new school. For a start it was housed in what seemed to me a huge red-brick Victorian building with a separate entrance for the girls on one side, and one for the boys on the other side. It was very different from the small single-storey school I went to in Bexleyheath at the end of our road. Also it was quite a walk to get to it. Still it turned out that I had no choice, as this was the only school I could attend. We all had to gather in the playground in the mornings, and when the bell went, we would all form into lines and file in one behind the other.

The local children didn't like the evacuees. They said we talked funny and that we were dirty and had fleas, which unfortunately happened to be true about some of us. They objected to us being in their school. 'You should go back to where you belong,' they told us. They loved to make fun of us and the boys were always fighting each other. Thelma finished school later in the day than me, which meant hanging around waiting for her. One day I walked past a group of local children. As I passed, one small boy dropped the apple he was eating. As I walked on I overheard him say to the others, 'She made me drop my apple, let's get her!' I started to run towards the bicycle sheds. By the time I had reached them, about five children cornered me, and surrounded me. I started to wheeze as the children crept closer and began to taunt me. I cowered at the threatening looks on their faces. One boy spat at me. 'You are stupid!' and as tears filled my eyes, 'she's crying, you're a baby, bye baby bunting!' They chanted pointing their fingers, 'You smell! You smell!'

Realising there was no way I could escape, it became harder to get my breath. I looked around helplessly wishing the ground would swallow me up. Just when I thought I would die, I spotted Thelma charging across the playground. When the children saw her they took off in the other direction. Saved at the last moment, I thought, and smiled a watery smile at her, relieved that she had seen what was going on. Thelma had just happened to be looking out of the classroom window to see if she could see me waiting, ever vigilant in her job to look after me, and had seen what was happening, so of course she came to my rescue. Thank goodness she had!

CHAPTER 5

Dolls, Diphtheria & Donkey Rides

Aunty Dora.

One day we were all gathered in the school hall. Parcels had arrived from the American servicemen stationed at the nearby air force base. Sitting on the hard polished floor with our legs crossed, we were very quiet as toys were pulled from a large box and handed out to us. First a wooden airplane, a train, and then the next toy to appear was a beautiful rag doll with a smiling face and big blue embroidered eyes. She had golden wool curls and a white muslin dress. Joy of joy! The headmistress, Mrs Josephs, called my name and handed it to me! I was over the moon. I had never had such a beautiful doll. As I cradled her in my arms, it was love at first sight. I named her Susan; she went everywhere with me, except to school, when she would sit on the bed awaiting my return.

Thelma and I became used to the new life we were living with the two ladies who had taken us in. Aunt Dora scrubbed out the hen shed for Thelma and I to play in, so we would pretend it was our own house. Many happy hours were spent with our toys in there. We didn't see much of Brian, who was thoroughly spoiled by his new foster parents. Unbeknown to them or us, he would play hooky from school and wander around the town. One day we had a visit from Major Hargreaves. He told us that Brian had become very ill and was in hospital. 'I am afraid he has Diphtheria,' he told us gravely, 'and he is very poorly.' Brian had been taken to hospital and put in an isolation unit, which meant that we could not visit him. The Major and his wife had showered him with toys and books. These were all burned in case of the spread of infection. We were all very worried about him. We knew that Thelma's twin, Diane, had died of Diphtheria when she was two.

A letter was sent to inform Mummy and Daddy. When it arrived at Pelham Road, Daddy opened it and quickly sent off a letter to Mummy. She had by now decided that she needed to leave the heavy bombing of Bexleyheath with her two youngest children. There was just no let up in the bombardment with incendiaries, V1s and, all told, about five different types of bomb being directed at London and surrounding areas, indeed the whole of the south-east corner of England and the London area was under fire. So together with David and Christopher, my mother had made her way north to the coal mining town of Wakefield and was taken in by a miner and his wife. They had a twelve-year-old daughter who was very spoiled. When Mummy received Daddy's letter, she decided that she would pay us a visit, and thereby visit Brian in the hospital as well. So while the miner and his wife kindly looked after David and Christopher, she came to see us.

It was Saturday, and Thelma and I were eagerly waiting for our mother to arrive. The Aunts had bought us some new clothes using both theirs and our clothing coupons, so we were feeling very smart in our new frocks. I had a new pink ribbon in my short hair and my buttoned shoes were polished. Thelma had a new floral cotton dress and matching ribbons on the end of her long plaits. I couldn't keep still and kept rushing to the window to see if Mummy was coming. Aunty Dora smiled at my impatience but knew it was pointless to tell me to sit down and read a book. After all, my Mummy was coming to see us!

At last there was a knock at the door, and when Aunt Dora went to open it, there stood my mother looking thin, pale and tired. She was wearing a brown tweed coat with leather buttons that looked like footballs, and a brown felt hat. She had on brown shoes and her wool stockings were wrinkled. Dora showed her into the back room where Thelma ran and hugged her. For some reason after all my excitement I felt shy of my mother and held back, until she put out her hand to me. Then, as I held her rough work-worn hand, she was just as I remembered her again, and I threw myself at her. She hugged and kissed me and stroked my hair, and it felt wonderful.

I sat on Mummy's lap as she sipped a cup of warming tea from one of the Aunts' pretty china tea cups and told us all about our younger brothers, and our sisters. Sheila was now working for the fire service with Daddy, who was also an air-raid warden, which meant that he had to go out at night and make sure that no lights were showing through the blackouts, giving directions to German planes. Betty was hoping to join the Wrens but in the meantime had joined the Women's Land Army to help the farmers with the harvest. Now that all the men had gone away to fight, there was a shortage of farm labour so women all over the country were being recruited to work with the farmers. Aunt Dora turned on the wireless. Vera Lynn was singing:

There'll be bluebirds over the white cliffs of Dover,
Tomorrow, just you wait and see.

There'll be love and laughter and peace ever after
Tomorrow, when the world is free.

That song still brings tears to my eyes and a lump to my throat even after sixty-five years. Mummy dabbed at her eyes and blew her nose. She told us that she had just come from the hospital where she had been visiting Brian. She had been so relieved to learn that he was making a good recovery. We were all very happy to learn that. Hooray!

We showed our mother where we slept, and the pretty bedroom the Aunts had prepared for us, then we all sat down for tea. Aunt Adelia had baked some of her Lancashire teacakes and the wonderful aroma wafted through the house. We had them hot with margarine. As Mummy sipped her weak tea she thanked the Aunts for taking such good care of us. The afternoon just flew by and then suddenly she was gone again. I felt lost once more and went up to our bedroom. Why couldn't she stay? I wondered to myself. Thelma came and found me lying on the bed cuddling Susan and crying quietly. She hugged me.

'You have to be brave,' she said kindly, 'we will soon be home and all together again.'

The two Aunts appeared at the bedroom door, seeing that we had both disappeared upstairs. They guessed how Thelma and I must have been feeling.

'Joost remember,' said Aunt Dora smiling brightly, 'there's a good time cooming, but it's a good time cooming!' Aunt Adelia joined in with, 'but it's a good time cooming', and they both started to laugh. I managed a watery smile and we all went downstairs.

The Aunts decided that Thelma and I needed something to take our minds off our homesickness, so Aunt Adelia offered to show Thelma how to crochet. Thelma had admired all the crocheted lace doilies throughout the house. Aunt Adelia presented Thelma with a crochet hook and some cotton. 'We will start with the chain stitch until you are familiar with holding the hook.' I was given a book of paper dolls and a pair of scissors. I had to cut out the clothes for the dolls. One doll looked like Shirley Temple, the famous child film star, with her head full of curls. She had some lovely frocks and hats. One was pale blue and covered in pink roses. There was a paper straw hat with daisies on to match and a little bag, which I placed on her wrist. The two dolls were on the covers of the book and you had to press them out first.

The Aunts looked at each other and smiled. They could see that their idea of getting us interested in something else had stopped us thinking about home – well, for a while anyway. Thelma got on well with her crochet and as she progressed, I decided that I wanted to learn as well but Aunt Adelia said she thought it would be too difficult for me so she would show me how to knit instead and then I could make some clothes for my doll. I quite liked that idea and couldn't wait to learn.

Like my sister, I also learned quite quickly and would lie on my back on the rug in front of the fire with my legs in the air, knitting a scarf for my doll. Aunt Dora remarked that it wasn't a very ladylike thing to do, but I just giggled and carried on; I was comfortable in that strange position. The day soon came when Brian was fully recovered from his sickness and he was allowed home. He was coming to pay us a visit, so Thelma and I rushed home from school to see him. Thelma and I had been assigned a cupboard in the front room for our toys and books that we had been accumulating from the Aunts and their friends, and I was just dying to show Brian my new things. But he arrived before I got home from school. I was so disappointed to find him already going through the cupboard and playing with my possessions. 'I wanted to show you them!' I shouted, feeling cheated. Brian looked up and laughed. I wanted to hit him but it was so nice to see him again that I hugged him instead.

If it was possible, he looked even thinner than when I last saw him, and his face was very white with all the time he had spent inside the hospital. 'Gerroff!' he said tugging at my arms. It was good to be together with him again. We played happily together until teatime and after tea his foster parents took him home, just as I was getting used to having him around again. People always seemed to be leaving, I thought to myself. I didn't like the empty feeling I had again. I wasn't sure why I missed Brian so much – after all, we used to fight a lot – but I suppose we were closer than I had realised.

The following day at school we were all assembled in the hall. After singing the hymn and having prayers, our headmistress stood on the platform in front of the whole school, looking very grim. She waited as we settled on the floor with our legs crossed. 'Now children, I want you to all listen very carefully,' she began, pushing a stray lock of her hair away from her eyes. Then Mrs Josephs went on to tell us that an evacuee who had been missing had been found. The police had been called out to search for her, she told us. Apparently she had gone for a walk by herself, along the towpath of the local canal that ran through the town. Sadly the child had slipped into the water and drowned. There was silence as we all took it in. The next words filled me with dread as Mrs Josephs continued, 'When they pulled her out, she was all bloated and blue and even her mother didn't recognise her.' Our headmistress felt that she had to educate us in the dangers of walking by the canal. So that none of us would be tempted to do it. But her words instilled in me fear of the danger of deep water, making me afraid of it for the rest of my life. That night I had nightmares and dreamed of swollen blue bodies floating in the dark muddy water.

Summer came without having had much contact with our parents or the rest of the family; they all seemed almost like strangers to us now, as we had settled into our new life with the Aunts in Padiham. Occasionally a letter or card would come in the mail, bringing the latest news from home. Day by day we grew to be very fond of the Aunts and they of us. Summer came and one day they announced that they were taking us on an outing to the seaside. Thelma and I were so excited we jumped up and down in delight; strange as it may seem, I had never seen the sea. How could you think about day trips with a war on? We caught a bus and then the train to Morcambe Bay. We were beside ourselves with anticipation to be going on an outing.

As the train puffed into the station the sun was shining and the birds were singing; it was going to be a lovely day! We found an empty carriage and I climbed in followed by Thelma, with the Aunts bringing up the rear. Thelma and I sat either side of the door so that we both had a window seat. As the train started to pick up speed, I almost nodded off with the gentle swaying of the carriage – but not quite.

We had brought our swimming things. Mummy had knitted my bathing suit. It was orange with yellow stripes. The Aunts carried a picnic packed in a square basket covered with a clean tea towel. My first glimpse of the sea was before we got off the train. Thelma saw it first. 'I can see the sea!' she announce excitedly. I followed her gaze and saw this vast expanse of water as far as the eye could see. It was sparkling as the sun shone and danced on the waves.

'We can see the sea, we can see the sea,' we chanted and jumped up and down until the Aunts, smiling, told us to sit down and be quiet. But we were so excited that we just couldn't sit still. The train puffed into Morcambe Station and we joined the other passengers as they shuffled along the platform.

Finally we got to the beach. I looked around at the other children already playing on the sand and building sand castles. The sea stretched to the horizon and the sunbeams danced upon the water. There was a wonderful fresh smell of salt and seaweed in the air. I breathed in deeply. Aunty Dora saw me. 'That's right, gel,' she said, 'breathe deeply, that air will do you good.' I wondered if we might see a mermaid and shaded my eyes with my hand as I looked out to sea. I had seen a picture in a book so I knew what to look for. Huge white gulls circled overhead, their loud raucous calls being carried away on the wind. Then they swooped down and plucked something from the waves. Thelma picked up a huge piece of bladder wrack seaweed and ran around in circles with it so that it trailed behind her in the wind.

I had never seen such a magical place and I gazed transfixed at the sunbeams dancing on the sea but to my disappointment no mermaid appeared. The Aunts bought us buckets and spades from a stand at the edge of the beach and after we had changed into our bathing suits, behind towels held up by the Aunts, we set to, building sand castles in the lovely soft sand. The Aunts settled themselves in deckchairs and took pleasure in watching our obvious enjoyment. Aunty Adelia reached for her knitting needles while Thelma and I held hands and ran together to the sea, to gather water in our buckets. Paddling along the edge, I ventured in a little further and began to jump up and down. Then I noticed that, as I jumped up, my knitted woollen costume, with the weight of the water in it, stretched and dropped down. I looked around embarrassed but no one had appeared to notice my near nakedness. I pulled it up over my chest.

We ran backwards and forwards to the sea with our buckets, collecting water for the castle moat, but as fast as we filled it of course, the water drained away. I found some white cockleshells and some delicate pink shells like tiny fingernails. As I turned them over in my hand I thought how pretty they were. Thelma discovered some limpets stuck to a rock. They were like little volcanoes. We prized them off with the edges of our metal spades, and after decorating the castle walls with them, we stood back and surveyed our handiwork, pleased with the result. I found a piece of stick and stuck it in the top as a flagpole.

Later, after the tide went out, leaving inviting little rock pools in its wake, we went for a walk along the beach and had a donkey ride. As the animal ambled along, its rough hair made the eczema at the back of my legs itch. The donkeys had their names printed on their bridles. Mine was called Lucky and Thelma's was Flo. The poor animals had spent the day walking up and down the beach giving rides and I think by the time we came to ride them they were worn out as they ambled along so very slowly, occasionally picking up speed as the donkey man jabbed them with a stick from behind, until Thelma frowned at him and said 'Don't do that! I don't mind if he is slow.' So he stopped jabbing the poor animal.

Finally when it was time to go home we boarded the train, with Thelma and I carrying a stick of shocking-pink peppermint rock with the word Morcambe printed all the way through the middle. I discovered that no matter how far you bit into it, there were the letters spelling Morcambe. We were tired but happy, chewing on the sweet sticky treat. The sea air, wind and sun had tangled our hair, put colour in our cheeks and turned our legs and arms pink. I snuggled up to Thelma, putting my head on her shoulder, and fell asleep as the train rocked gently to and fro along the track. I was dreaming of white-capped waves, sand and sun, mermaids, and sand castles covered in shells.

CHAPTER 6

Little Beasts

The summer holidays came to an end and it was time to go back to school again. We had had maybe two letters from Mummy and Daddy. Mummy had returned to Bexleyheath. While she was in Yorkshire, she had found a job in a munitions factory, leaving the boys with the Yorkshire miner's family while she worked. On her returning home earlier than usual one day, to her dismay, she found that David had been shut in the coal cupboard in the cellar and that, as he wouldn't stop crying, he was soaking wet from having had water poured over him to shut him up. My mother soon told the miner's wife what she thought of them, packed her bags and left. 'I gave them a piece of my mind! I would sooner put up with the bombs than have my boys ill-treated,' she announced to a surprised but delighted Daddy on reaching home with the boys. He was so happy to see her and the boys again and decided that they would just sit it out until the end of the war. After all, he reasoned, they had been spared so far, hadn't they?

It was Saturday and Thelma needed new shoes, so we caught the bus into Burnley. We were going shopping with the Aunts, and they bought her a pair of the traditional clogs worn by the children in Lancashire. As the streets were cobbled it made sense, but when we reached home, as Thelma tried them on again, she complained that the wooden shoes now hurt her feet, so Aunt Dora took them back and exchanged the clogs for some proper shoes; these cost much more but they could not have Thelma uncomfortable. The two ladies really were so caring. They wanted us to be happy and comfortable and would do anything to make sure that we were.

So that I would not feel left out, Aunt Dora bought me a brown cotton pixie hood with a red gingham lining. I hated both the colour and the shape but they made me wear it to school anyway. 'It will keep your ears warm,' they explained. So there was no arguing about it. I was now considered capable of coming home on my own from school without getting lost and on one particular day, while I was on my way home, I undid the ribbons of the pixie hood and walked along shaking my head, until the offending headgear fell off. Resisting the urge to look behind me, I carried on as though nothing had happened, feeling glad that I had got rid of the stupid hat and feeling very clever that I had devised such a plan. Unfortunately for me, I had only been home about five minutes when there was a knock at the door and a small boy stood there with my hat in his hand. He had been following me and had seen it fall off my head. I scowled at him and looked very sheepishly at Aunt Dora as she thanked him and took the hat. She gave me an old-fashioned sidelong look when I lied and declared that I hadn't realised it had fallen off my head. Somehow, I don't think she believed me.

The following week, the Aunts decided that it was time that they got rid of their old tin bathtub and got a proper fitted bath. So they had one plumbed into our bedroom.

It stood alongside the bed in the corner by the window; it would be so much easier now than having to lift pots of hot water to fill the old tin bath, and you could stretch out in it as well.

I was the first one to use the new bath. Thelma, having decided that I should have a bubble bath poured lots of Rinso soap flakes into the water. I thought it was wonderful and felt just like a film star, especially as she nearly filled the bath with water instead of having the customary 2 inches! I lay back, surrounded by the bubbles, and closed my eyes. What bliss! I felt cleaner than I had for a long time. Thelma washed my hair then I put on my nightdress, wrapped a towel around my head, and followed my sister downstairs to the dining room where the fire was burning merrily in the grate. The Aunts looked up as we came into the sitting room. 'That was so nice,' I said happily, feeling cosseted.

I removed the towel and began to scratch my head. I had been scratching my head quite a lot recently and as Aunt Dora was drying it for me with a towel, she let out a scream. 'Adelia, look at her head,' she shouted pointing, 'she's got nits!' So that was why I kept scratching. The Aunts had assumed that it was just my eczema bothering me again. Adelia quickly got a tin tray. I had to lean over the table backwards, and as Dora combed my hair with a fine-toothed metal comb the headlice landed on the tray and Adelia pounced on them squashing each one with her thumbnail. They made a cracking sound. Ugh!

Later the Aunts got some evil-smelling brown ointment and plastered my hair with it.

'To kill the little beasts,' Dora announced. 'Don't worry yersel, lass, we'll get rid of them,' she said as she tied a scarf around my head. 'So that the grease doesn't get on your pillow,' she explained. The next day, I was teased and taunted mercilessly at school, as everyone knew why my hair looked so greasy and was plastered to my head. Most of the children at some time or another had had nits – it was a real problem with the evacuees – and so everyone recognised the greasy condition of my hair. This was one time when I didn't mind wearing my horrible pixie hood and wished I could wear it in class! I complained to the Aunts that everyone was making fun of me, but all Aunt Dora would say was, 'Just tell whoever is teasing you that you got the fleas from them.'

Although I tried that, the response I got was, 'No you didn't, I don't have nits.' So I just had to put up with the jibes until the lice had gone and I could have the horrible ointment removed from my head. What a relief when my hair was back to normal.

The next weekend, Thelma decided that she would like to visit the cinema in town so she asked the Aunts if she could go with a girl friend. They told her that she could, but that she had to take me with her. There was a Walt Disney film showing and the Aunts assumed that that was the film she intended to see. Thelma, however, wanted to see *The Snake Pit*. She felt she was too adult to watch Walt Disney. So she and her friend took me to the other cinema. The sight of the snakes scared me half to death. I spent most of the time with my hands over my eyes and it resulted in more nightmares that night – though we never let on to the Aunts what we had seen.

On the Sunday Thelma and I, and four of her school friends, decided to go 'Oop Pendle Hill'. The sun was shining with the wind making it feel fresh, so we wore our coats and gloves. Pendle was a very high local hill and together we climbed to the top. Of course, I was puffing by the time we reached the summit. The view was just amazing but I felt cold, the wind was howling and tearing at our hair turning it into rats' tails. The girls found a hollow for me to sit in, and taking off their coats, they covered me up to keep me warm whilst they danced about together in the wind.

I felt so cosy amid the heather and gorse bushes that soon I was asleep, dreaming of a life that seemed so far away, where everything was scary and the noise was deafening, but where you hadn't to be scared because that might make something bad happen to you. You had to sing to keep up your spirits and laugh as though you didn't care. Then one day it might just all go away. Then you could laugh and really mean it. I awoke feeling chilled; the girls were tugging at their coats. 'Coom on!' Thelma shouted above the wind. 'It's time to go.'

She grabbed my arm and pulled me up. A lark was singing high in the sky, such a tiny speck, you could hardly see it. For the moment I didn't know where I was. Then the smell of the heather, the yellow gorse bushes and the wind brought me back to reality. With rosy cheeks and hair a tangle, we raced each other down the grassy hill, running so fast that we ended up rolling down and finished up in a tangled heap at the bottom laughing together uncontrollably. That was so much fun!

CHAPTER 7

Father Christmas

The days wore on and soon it would be Christmas. Thelma and I hadn't seen much of Brian and we had got used to this life, living with the Aunts. They had grown fond of us and we of them. Thelma had secretly been crocheting a mat to give them for Christmas. She said it would be from both of us. We had saved our pennies and bought Brian a scarf. We spent a Saturday afternoon wrapping our gifts, and putting paper chains together. The chains came in a stack of different-coloured paper strips with a sticky end, which you had to lick and join to the opposite end. Then the next strip was threaded through the loop and joined in the same way until you had a long chain to drape from one corner of the ceiling to the other.

Thelma and I surveyed our work with pride. Then Aunty Dora produced some paper bells she had been keeping in the attic from Christmases gone by. There were three bells and a globe. They were folded flat but when opened up became beautiful rainbow-coloured bells. I had never seen such pretty decorations. We grouped two of the bells together and hung them over the back door and put the other one with the globe in the corner of the ceiling, joined by the chains. To complete the look, a bunch of mistletoe hung from the ceiling lamp.

Soon it was Christmas Eve. Aunt Dora asked me if I would like to hang up a pillowcase for Father Christmas to fill. I gave her an old-fashioned look.

'That would be far too big,' I said, 'we always hang a stocking at home.' I was remembering the Christmases we spent at home and the lovely crackly noise the stretchy, parcel-filled stocking made in the early hours of the morning. Then, the delight in opening the small parcels containing colouring books or hankies, then finding an apple, then a nut in the toe, right at the end of the stocking.

'Well,' Aunt Dora replied, winking at Adelia, 'we doon't have any spare stockings so it will joost have to be a pillowcase.' So Thelma and I took the pillowcases and hung them at the end of the bed.

'Our toys will get lost in there, if we get any,' Thelma whispered to me in bed later. There was no answer; I was already asleep.

I awoke early on a very chilly Christmas morning. It was just becoming light as I stretched and sat up, scratching my head and yawning. Then I remembered what day it was and peered through the gloom to the end of the bed, now with the excited expectation of what Father Christmas might have left me. Pushing back the quilt, I crawled to the end of the bed and looked over the foot. I couldn't believe my eyes. Not only had he been, but also, I could see that my pillowcase was bulging with toys. 'Thelma, look!' I cried in wonder, bouncing up and down in my excitement. Thelma rubbed her eyes sleepily and sat up, then took a flying leap to the end of the bed, which bounced me into the air. I laughed at her expression, as she spotted her pillowcase and her eyes grew wide with amazement.

She was as surprised as I was at all the presents we had received.

The noise we were making quickly brought the Aunts running from their room; they didn't want to miss any of the fun of seeing us open the gifts they had lovingly placed in the pillowcases. We all went downstairs so that we could unwrap the rest of our parcels in comfort, in the living room. Quickly we ripped the paper off the many parcels, which the Aunts had wrapped for us. Amongst my gifts were several books. One was from Mummy and Daddy. It was a book of fairy stories and had a picture of a unicorn on the front. How I treasured it! Thelma also received a book from our parents. We both had socks and hankies. Aunt Adelia had made the socks and embroidered flowers in the corners of the hankies. Thelma had a set of crochet hooks and I had some wool and knitting needles.

Brian arrived after breakfast with Major Hargreaves and his wife. They were to share our Christmas dinner with us. Brian told us that he too had hung a pillowslip and among his gifts were a train set and some toy soldiers. He had brought the soldiers with him. They came in a long cardboard box, were made of lead and dressed like guardsmen, with lovely red jackets and tall black busby hats. Two of the Aunts' hens had been slaughtered for dinner. The feathers, having been carefully plucked, were saved to stuff a cushion.

The mouth-watering smell of roast chicken filled the little house. We had a lovely Christmas dinner, with crackers to pull. (I can't imagine where the Aunts had found those.) Each one contained a paper hat and a small novelty. All of us wearing paper hats, we hungrily tucked into the roast chicken, with bread sauce and stuffing, lovely crispy roast potatoes, carrots and Brussels sprouts with thick dark brown gravy. What a feast! There was Christmas pudding and custard to follow, together with some mince pies that the Hargreaveses had brought with them. Aunt Adelia had made the wonderful fruity pudding; she had put silver threepenny pieces inside for some lucky person to find and so we had to watch how we ate it, in case we broke a tooth! She had saved up all her and Aunt Dora's ration coupons together with some of ours, and had managed to get some dried fruit for it. Afterwards, feeling fuller than we had felt for a long time, and with a lovely cosy feeling, we sat by the fire and sang carols together:

Oh little town of Bethlehem, how still we see thee lie,
Above thy deep and dreamless sleep the silent stars go by.
But in thy dark streets shineth, the everlasting light
The hopes and fears of all the years, are met in thee tonight.

And we sang 'Silent night, Holy night'. By the time Brian and his foster parents left, it had begun to snow, and as I looked through the window, I noticed everything sparkling with ice crystals under the street lights. Just like a Christmas card – how pretty! It had been one of the best Christmases ever, but even so, Thelma, Brian and I had missed our parents and our other brothers and sisters. It certainly was a different Christmas this year. I wondered how much longer we would have to be away from our home and family.

CHAPTER 8

Coming Home

Brian, Thelma and Wendy.

Winter slowly faded into spring. Finally, as the saying goes, the March winds and April showers brought forth the May flowers. Then one day we learned that we were to be going home. The war was not over but it was deemed safe for us to return – our brave airmen with the help of the Canadians and Americans had begun to turn the tide and our parents wanted us home again. The Aunts gave us the news, at the same time looking rather sad. Thelma turned a beaming face on me and we hugged each other tightly. The Aunts were happy for us but said how much they were going to miss having us stay. We had become a part of their lives – just as they were part of ours. We would always be grateful for the love and care they had shown us. Much later we heard that many other evacuees had not been so lucky and had been mistreated and even abused, so we were very fortunate in having been placed with two such kind and caring ladies.

The week before we were to leave, we were taken to the local park to have our photos taken. The three of us stood side by side in our best clothes, our shoes shone. Brian had a new grey lumber jacket and short trousers, whilst Thelma and I wore the dresses the Aunts had bought for us. I had my hair cut into a short bob with a ribbon bow. I wouldn't smile. Now I didn't want to leave this place. It felt so safe. Why was everything always changing, just as we got used to it? How confusing life could be.

On the day that we were to leave, the sun shone, in complete contrast to the day when we had arrived. The Aunts, and the Major and his wife, came with us all to the station to see us off and I clutched my beloved rag doll Susan. This time we had a case each to hold all the belongings we had acquired while we had been away. We were to be travelling with many of the children who had arrived with us on that day so long ago. This time there was such an air of joy coupled with sadness at the thought of leaving our new friends and then lots of laughing as we played tag, up and down the platform.

As the train puffed into the station, I held tightly to Thelma's hand, and together with Brian, we found a carriage where we could all sit together. The journey we took so long ago to escape the bombs was a journey into the unknown. Now, however, we knew what we were going to find at the end of this trip – our family – and it was hard to contain the happiness we felt.

We hung out of the train window and waved to the Aunts and the Hargreaveses until the train went into a tunnel. We were never to see them again. The children began throwing things at each other, jumping on the seats, and chasing up and down the carriage, just as they did when we arrived. When they tired of that, they sat and looked out of the windows. The countryside raced by, fields and woodlands came and went until we were on the outskirts of London. We became silent and our faces grew serious as we gazed at the devastation. The huge bomb craters, piles of rubble, burned-out cars and broken furniture everywhere. Pale and thin, strangely haunted-looking people standing silently looking at where their homes had been, flattened to dust whilst the occupants had stayed safe in the bomb shelters or underground stations. We had forgotten the horrors of war whilst we were away, and now it was all coming flooding back. So many bombs had been dropped, transforming rows of houses to piles of bricks and dirt everywhere. People's lives had been disrupted and ruined, changing them forever.

As we reached Bexleyheath, I began to feel afraid again. I found myself listening for the siren and looked warily skywards, but I couldn't see any planes. The train slowly puffed into the station. A sea of hope-filled faces gazed out of the carriage windows, searching for someone or something familiar. Sadly some people were missing and of course we were all a little older and hopefully wiser. We felt that nothing would be the same, and it was a scary feeling.

Thelma, Brian and I grabbed our belongings and pushed and shoved like all the other children trying to get off the train first. Bursting forth through the narrow carriage doors in a rush to find someone familiar, the children spilled onto the platform to be pounced on and hugged by their waiting parents. We looked around and, further down the platform, Brian spotted Mummy wearing the familiar brown tweed coat with the leather football buttons. She had a green scarf tied around her head. 'Come on!' he cried. 'There she is!' Brian dropped his case and took off in excitement, up the platform, leaving us to pick up his bag.

We ran after him hampered by our bulging bags, and then I saw Mummy looking somehow smaller and thinner than I had remembered. She saw us at the same time and stood with her arms out wide, ready to gather us all up. 'Look at you all,' she exclaimed, 'haven't you grown. I would hardly have recognised you.' It was obvious to her that we had eaten well. We had all gained weight and were in good health. Mummy steered us out of the station to where a fleet of red London Transport buses stood, ready to take us all home. We joined the queue of happy smiling children and adults all so overjoyed to be reunited at last!

'Where are David and Christopher?' asked Thelma. 'Are they alright?'

'Yes,' Mummy replied, smiling happily, 'I have left them with Mrs Clayton. They are both fine and can't wait to see you all.'

As we boarded the bus everyone seemed to be smiling and laughing, seemingly oblivious to the fresh bomb sites all around us; maybe they were just too used to them. The bus had to make a few detours around the roads that were now impassable but then we reached the clock tower – there it still stood in all its glory. Still untouched by the bombs that had fallen all around. The clock struck three. Mummy helped us off the bus. 'It's nearly time for tea,' she said, putting her arm around Brian and happily surveying her brood, like a mother hen.

Together we made our way down Woolwich Road carrying our bags, occasionally stopping to change hands. There didn't appear to be any more bomb sites here. Mummy noticed that we were still wearing our luggage labels on our coats. 'Precious parcels,' Doris said. She was so happy to have her children back. However, the change in our accents made her smile – we had all come home with Lancashire accents! A chilly wind was blowing as we turned the corner into Pelham Road. We hastened our steps as we reached the last phase of our long journey. Brian broke into a run and stood jumping from one foot to the other, waiting for us at the gate to number 14, his socks around his ankles. 'Hurry up, I need to go to the lavatory!' I didn't know where he got the energy. I was feeling very tired.

'Wait a minute,' Mummy said going into number 10. 'We have to pick up David and Christopher.' She knocked on the door.

Mrs Clayton threw open her door with a big beaming smile on her face. She was carrying Christopher on her arm and David clutched at her skirt, sucking his thumb and peeping out at us shyly. 'Welcome home!' she cried.

'I won't come in,' said Mummy, 'we all need the lavatory, and it was a long wait!' she added as she took the boys from Elsie. David looked at us, and then he smiled. Mummy had told him we were coming home and he had remembered us!

'Alright then,' replied Elsie Clayton, 'I will talk to you later.' Turning to us she said, 'Haven't you all grown! It's so nice to have you home again.' With that she closed the door.

As we approached our home I glanced across the road at the bomb site. The rubble had been cleared away and a wooden fence to keep people out now surrounded the site. But I didn't want to think about that. I was concerned about Christopher. He seemed huge and he looked different. Mummy opened the door with one hand, at the same time balancing Christopher on her hip. The place seemed much smaller than I remembered. We went into the front room. I looked around. It seemed very scruffy compared with the Aunts' home. There was a smell of stale food. The hole was still in the linoleum on the floor, and though the windows had been repaired for the umpteenth time, the curtains were still torn from the broken glass. Also the window sill seemed to have got closer to the floor, or so it appeared to me, as I had got taller. My attention turned to Christopher.

'That is not Christopher,' I announced firmly.

'Well, who do you think it is?' my mother replied with a smile.

'I don't know,' I said, my voice shaking. Being so tired, I was very close to tears. I couldn't understand what was going on. Why didn't my baby brother look the same as when we left?

Thelma laughed. 'The fairies took Christopher, and left us a Changeling.' Then, 'Of course it is Christopher,' she continued. 'He has just grown, that's all.'

'Don't tease her,' Mummy said. 'Come and say hello to him,' she said grabbing my hand and drawing me to her.

I went and looked closer. The baby looked at me and smiled and somehow he looked familiar again. Well maybe it was Christopher, but he certainly had changed a lot from the tiny infant I had last seen. His golden fuzz of hair had become lovely golden curls, and he had freckles on his little nose and his legs and arms had got longer and plumper.

'Put the kettle on, Thelma,' my mother said happily, 'we will have a cup of tea and then you can tell me all about your adventures. There are some broken biscuits in the tin.

Mr Jacobs let me have them cheap.' Mr Jacobs, manager of the Home and Colonial grocer's, would sell loose biscuits by the dozen and any that were broken were sold much cheaper. I blew a raspberry at Christopher and he laughed. I laughed too and ruffled his curls. He looked like a cherub and was wearing pale-green rayon knickers and a white shirt with a Peter Pan collar. On his chubby feet he wore little fabric sandals. He could walk now, if a little shakily, and I marvelled as I saw him move around the room hanging onto the chairs. When he reached Daddy's desk he began to play with the knobs, talking to himself. David, not to be outdone, joined him. David was taller now, more like a little boy and less of a baby. They chuckled together.

'Look, Tritita,' David said as he bashed the knobs against the wood. He couldn't manage to say Christopher. These two boys had grown very close, as they had stayed together, in the same way that I grew closer to Thelma. David and Christopher would always be close in years to come.

Meanwhile, Brian had disappeared upstairs to survey what was still there of the belongings he had left behind. Mummy and I, with Thelma bringing up the rear, decided to follow him. We found him curled up on his bed crying. He had ruled the roost with his foster parents and they had thoroughly spoiled him. Now he knew this would stop and he would be just one of seven children again. Mummy sat on his bed and stroked his hair; she was happy to have her firstborn son home again.

'Don't cry,' she said kindly, 'I know it all seems strange to you but you will soon get used to us again.' She turned to me, and said, 'You will be sleeping in this room too now,' pointing to the single bed on the other side of the

8-foot-wide room, the only other piece of furniture in there. Both beds were covered with dark-grey army surplus blankets and topped with khaki Land Army coats for extra warmth. There were no pretty pink eiderdowns in our house (although our parents had an old threadbare golden yellow eiderdown on their bed). It transpired that David and Christopher would be sleeping in a cot and chair-bed in our parents' front bedroom while Sheila, Betty and Thelma would be in the double bed in the third bedroom. Mummy took both our hands as Brian sat up. 'Come on, let's go and have that tea,' she said cheerfully. 'I have made some cheese scones as well to have with it.'

Sitting at the table with my jam jar of tea warming my hands, I began to feel butterflies in my stomach and myself getting nervous. I was thinking that now that we were home again we had better get ready for the air-raid warning to go any time. 'Will the bombs be dropping soon?' I asked Thelma, who was sitting beside me as we sipped our tea and nibbled on the lovely fresh-tasting scones. Mummy had put a scraping of butter and margarine on them; she liked to mix the National Butter with the Stork margarine to make it go further.

'I don't know,' Thelma replied, looking enquiringly at Mummy.

'Things are getting better now,' my mother answered looking concerned. 'They don't drop so often now, otherwise we wouldn't have had you home,' she added. I didn't feel convinced, and as we chatted, telling our mother all about the things we had done and the things we had seen, our visit to the seaside and the pillowcases we had that Father Christmas had filled, I still half expected to hear the old familiar wail of the siren.

Betty was away with the Land Army down in Sittingbourne in Kent. Daddy and Sheila were still working together; when they came home it was so wonderful to see them again. We all fell upon Daddy, hugging him and kissing him. He looked very happy as he gazed around the crowded room at his now once more almost complete family. 'Haven't you all grown!' he said. 'I have been waiting for this day for a long time,' he announced happily. Mummy had made a huge casserole of macaroni cheese for tea, and with Christopher in his high chair pulled up to the table, and David sitting on Sheila's lap, we laughed and chatted and ate hungrily, scraping our plates until they were almost clean. Brian's was clean as he licked it to get every last scrap. Our father sat at the head of the table pulling faces, wiggling his bushy black eyebrows and making us laugh more. He beamed at us as we fell about laughing at his antics. Oh, it was so good to be together and able to laugh again, and the siren didn't sound once.

Once we had washed and cleaned our teeth and were all ready for bed, Daddy got up and went over to the desk; he opened the top drawer and brought out a Mars bar. Cutting it into slices he handed one to each of us. The tiny sliver of chocolate tasted so good. Finally we went to bed. I felt very happy that we hadn't heard the wailing of the air-raid siren and that we were all together again.

After an uneventful night, the next morning when I awoke I was scratching myself. There were red marks on my arms and legs. I leapt out of bed and screamed as I noticed a round flat red beetle on my pillow. Brian sat up quickly. 'Wot's wrong?' he enquired sleepily.

'There is something in my bed, did you put it there?' I accused him. Brian got out of bed to investigate, and hearing me yell, Mummy came running from her room. I pointed to the offending creature that obligingly didn't move.

'Oh no,' she said, trying to get hold of the beetle, 'it's a bed bug!' I looked at her in dismay. It turned out that bed bugs had taken up residence in the cracks in the walls, between the wall and the skirting board or door post and they would come out at night to feed on you, sucking your blood and leaving red and itchy weals. My father put some DDT powder in a pump spray and went round puffing it into all the cracks.

'There,' he announced with satisfaction, 'that should get rid of the little beggars.'

My mother took me into the bathroom and made me sit on the linen box while she rubbed the red areas with the evil-smelling mustard-coloured TCP ointment. I hated the smell of that stuff but it was a cure for everything and really did work well. Mummy swore by it. 'There,' she said, putting the screw top back on the tube, and washing her hands. 'That will be better soon. Try not to scratch.' The red marks together with the bed bugs soon disappeared and in the next days and weeks we fell back into the rhythm of going to school. There were fewer air raids now. We didn't need to go down into the shelter, so consequently tempers were less frayed as we managed to achieve a full night's sleep.

Finally we received the tremendous news that the war was finally over. We had been sitting huddled around the radio when we heard. Oh, how we cheered. VE Day – Victory in

Europe at last! We had won the war against Germany and Hitler was dead! Hooray! Now we could continue our lives without the incessant interruption and uncertainty of what would happen each day.

It was decided that we would have a street party to celebrate. In towns up and down the length and breadth of England, it was the same story; it was time to have some fun again! So parties were planned. We were going to have the biggest celebration ever! The lamp posts were hung with red, white and blue bunting, and Union Jacks fluttered from the windows of every house. Tables and chairs were set up down the length of the street with everyone providing some food for the festivity. We had sandwiches, cakes, jelly and blancmange. Such a spread – we hadn't seen so much food for ages. The men attached loudspeakers to the lamp posts to relay the music to the whole street. We put on our glad rags and sang and danced. Then we sat down and ate our fill. Brian made himself sick with too many cream cakes – but who could blame him for that? When the food was gone, we started to sing and dance again, and forming a long line, and winding in and out of the tables, we danced the conga, and after the conga we did the Lambeth Walk and we all sang:

> When you go down Lambeth way,
> Any evening any day,
> You'll find them all
> Doing the Lambeth Walk
> Oi!

Three cheers for the King and Queen!

Hip, hip, hooray! Hip, hip, hooray! Hip, hip, hooray! Oh how we cheered and hugged each other, as we partied late into the night. Until, tired and happy, we all went home to our beds. At last our lives could get back to normal, whatever that was! I had yet to find out what a normal life meant.